Lanesboro
MINNESOTA

Its Past, Places and People

By
Steve Harris

Illustrated by Lisa Gaunky
Foreword by Theo St. Mane
Cover Painting by Chip Borkenhagen

LISA G.
2016

First Edition: May, 2018
Copyright 2018, Steve Harris
All rights reserved

This activity is made possible by the voters of Minnesota through a grant
from the Southeastern Minnesota Arts Council thanks to a legislative
appropriation from the Arts & Cultural Heritage Fund.

ISBN: 978-0-9989116-4-9

Published by

40274 Diamond Lake Street
Aitkin, MN 56431
218.851.4843
www.riverplacepress.com
chip@riverplacepress.com

For more information about Lanesboro, Minnesota, including business, lodging, theater, and restaurant guides, please visit:

www. Lanesboro.com

For additional copies of this book–"Lanesboro, Minnesota" by Steve Harris–contact Steve at sharrislb@gmail.com or call (952) 836-7904.

Dedication

To Susie

My best friend, my partner, my love.
"I bet you could do a B & B," I said. I was right.
You've done it beautifully.

Thanks for all the ways you made our
Lanesboro dream come true.

Table of Contents

Table of Contents

"Lanesboro is a series of simple pleasures."

My neighbor, Vern

Foreword

Steve Harris includes in the pages of his heartwarming and ingenious book the sentiment, "Lanesboro is a series of simple pleasures." Nothing, in my opinion, could be truer.

Having grown up in Lanesboro, Minnesota, I experienced firsthand a great many of the simple pleasures this magical little town has to offer.

Childhood pleasures of 'going out to play' without the need for adult supervision, ranging with my friends through nearby woods and ravines, eating rhubarb straight from a neighbor's patch, returning to the unlocked doors of home as the sun dipped toward the horizon and my mother called our names from the back window. A part of a community where each child was known and accounted for by the whole – "you're one of the St. Mane boys, aren't you?"

"Yes ma'am."

Simple pleasures for child and adult alike. To be part of a group, to be known and recognized, to see and feel the kind regard of others, to live in a place of beauty, to be proud of your community and to feel a desire to contribute as you see those around you contributing....Lanesboro has provided me all these pleasant experiences and more.

Knowing that so many others also feel a special kinship with this little village in the valley is also a pleasure.

The draw to Lanesboro's quiet sublimity is not new. For generations travelers have discovered and rediscovered the tranquil views of forest, bluff and river, and enjoyed the geniality of the local populace. Today that trend continues as thousands of annual visitors journey here for recreation, theater, shopping, sightseeing, and other peaceful pursuits. Those who are open to really seeing the world around them discover a place full of simple pleasures. The kind found in unhurried strolls, savored ice cream, browsing, laughter, good food, the appreciation of history, and the slow regard of artful things.

Enjoy the simple pleasures of Lanesboro!

Theo St. Mane
Author (with Don Ward), *"Images of America: Lanesboro, Minnesota"*
Author, *"Images of America: Rochester, Minnesota"*

What Brings You to Town?

"Sooner or later everybody seems to end up in Lanesboro."
Heidi Dybing

Maybe this is your first visit here. You've come with your spouse, family or friends for a day or weekend to bike, see a play, maybe tube the Root River. Or just relax. Good for you. You've made a great choice.

Perhaps you come here often. You do all those fun things. You already know how this little town can surprise you with all it has to explore and enjoy. Go for it!

Maybe you live here—or used to. You have roots here. Lucky you. You know better than anyone what Lanesboro feels like and why people are drawn here.

Whatever brings you here, for however long your stay, know that you're in a special place. A unique and beautiful place. An inspiring place. A place that somehow leaves a delightful, even magical mark on people long after they leave.

Through brief stories and the beautiful line drawings of Lisa Gaunky, this book will help you discover Lanesboro, Minnesota—its past, places and people. You'll learn why this little town is still thriving after 150 years. Maybe some of its inspiring magic will even rub off on you along the way. That's worth a trip right there.

Before we begin, keep a few things in mind. We'll explore history in these pages, but not in a text-book sort of way. We'll visit special places, but certainly not all of them. We'll meet people from long ago and today, but only a small sampling. Think of this book as more of a painting of Lanesboro than a photograph.

To "paint" Lanesboro is to capture a moving target. People come and go, businesses open and close, town life changes, as it does everywhere. What I describe in places may no longer fit your current Lanesboro experience. (An example? Gordie no longer bakes one-a-day pies at the Spud Boy Diner. Our loss!) That's okay. New discoveries and joys replace the old. I hope this book helps you discover this town through your own eyes, too. Lucky you.

Welcome to Lanesboro!

Steve Harris, January, 2018

When Minnesota became a state in 1858 more people lived in Fillmore County than in any other Minnesota county. That remained true until 1870.

The Roads Leading Here

Many things draw people to Lanesboro. At least one of them is inspiration.

Lanesboro, Minnesota, population 754, is more village than town. It's located in southeastern Minnesota at the convergence of Minnesota Highways 250 and 16 and Fillmore County Road 8, all good roads, but you still need to hunt a bit to find this place. A few challenging curves on the final miles here make just-passing-through traffic pretty rare. Lanesboro is a destination. You have to want to get here.

Many people do. On a summer weekend the town's population nearly triples. In a typical busy season (April through October) more than 25,000 tourists will visit Lanesboro. They'll make their way here from all over Minnesota and the Midwest, from many states, even from other countries.

Why do all those people come? Why do we see so many day-trippers, campers and sightseers here? Why have many bought weekend get-away or retirement houses here? And why are the lucky people who live in Lanesboro so proud to call it home?

Some of the "roads" that bring people to Lanesboro are obvious. One is the glowing attention this town regularly receives in local, state, even national media. Lanesboro recently ranked #3 on USA Today's list of "10 Best Midwestern Small Towns." Similar honors pop up all over.

- "One of the 50 Best Small Downtowns" (Best Choice Reviews)
- "One of the 20 Best Small Towns in the Country to Visit" (Smithsonian Magazine)
- "One of 25 Underrated Midwestern Towns You Should Visit" (Fodors)
- "One of America's Prettiest Towns" (Forbes Traveler)
- "One of 40 American Towns You Haven't Heard of But Should Visit ASAP" (House Beautiful)
- "One of the 50 Most Adorable Small Towns in America" (LoveExploring)

People hear all that and get curious. They want to see what all the fuss is about. They head here to check it out for themselves. But it's more than internet lists or homey titles that attract people to Lanesboro. What is it exactly?

Let's start by just looking around. It's beautiful here. A small village nestled in a little valley, surrounded by thick woods, towering bluffs, and rolling hills, with an historic downtown, iconic church steeples, classic railroad bridges and a robust river running through it, is hard to resist.

It's also a fun place. People come to Lanesboro to play. Bikers trek here by the thousands to pedal the Root River Trail, one of the most popular and family-friendly bike trails in the Midwest. Others take to the river in canoes, inner tubes and kayaks. Lanesboro offers fine restaurants, unique shops, a vibrant art scene (including the Commonweal Theatre, a local professional troupe with a 30-year history and a national reputation). People fish, golf, hike, and cross-country ski in Lanesboro. If you like to play, this place delivers.

Lanesboro's history is another attraction. Visit its authentic 19th century downtown or its historic neighborhoods of beautifully-restored homes and you can step back in time. Stories of how the town started and the colorful people who've also walked these streets (Buffalo Bill, for one) are fun to hear. People come just for that.

Other "roads" bring people to Lanesboro. They come to visit Amish country, explore nearby caves and state parks, eat homemade pie (this is Minnesota, after all), and generally soak in the quiet pace and friendly faces of small town America.

Yes, that's all very hard to resist, and people come here for all of those obvious attractions. But there's something deeper going on, if you ask me. I've lived here for nearly a decade. My wife, Susie, and I are innkeepers at a Lanesboro bed & breakfast. We've met thousands of people who made a deliberate choice to spend time here for a day, a weekend or longer. We know families who've called this place home for decades, even generations.

I ask questions, I listen, I learn. Why do people come to Lanesboro? Beautiful scenery, fun things to do, colorful history—all of that for sure. But there's more. I say you can sum it up in the word "inspiring." Lanesboro, Minnesota, is an inspiring place.

"Inspiration," says social analyst David Brooks, "is a thrilling feeling of elevation, a burst of energy, an awareness of enlarged possibilities." Lanesboro helps people feel those things. Somehow this place relaxes and energizes people at the same time. Many say the natural beauty here does that. Others point to people here who encourage and ignite creativity. Whatever the source, and perhaps there's a bit of mystery in all this, this place is inspiring.

That goes way back. This town has inspiration in its DNA. Lanesboro didn't just happen. In the 1860s a small group of people from far away got so taken by the area—inspired, we might say—that they decided to build a town here. Working with settlers already in the valley, their combined vision, hard work and perseverance pulled it off. Maybe some of that early inspiration still lingers today.

Many roads lead to Lanesboro. When people arrive they find themselves surprised, delighted even, by a little town with a look and feel—and an inspiration—all its own. How does that happen? Let me start by telling you how it happened to me.

On a summer day as many as 1,100 canoers, tubers, and kayakers are on the Root River.

Gertrude, You'd Love This Place

"This place is magical," I said, after being here 15 minutes.

The author Gertrude Stein got into hot water by saying her hometown of Oakland, California, had "no 'there' there." I think Gertrude would love Lanesboro. Why? Because there's a "there" here. An unmistakable sense of place. You feel it immediately when you arrive. You remember it long after you leave.

I saw Lanesboro for the first time on a summer day in August, 2007. I drove here from my home in Minneapolis with my then girlfriend (later wife) Susie for two reasons. The first was to check out a bed & breakfast for sale. The second was to see southeastern Minnesota for the first time.

I grew up in California but have lived in Minnesota for more than thirty years. I'd driven the 35W north-south interstate dozens of times. The farthest place south I'd actually seen, though, was the city of Rochester. That seemed far enough. Minnesota's best scenery is up north, right? Everybody knows that.

Before planning our Lanesboro visit I'd never heard of it. Google told me it was a small town about 130 miles southeast of the Twin Cities. A few big cornfields shy of Iowa apparently. What could be worth seeing there? Our trip was feeling like little more than a lark, but that was fine. Larks can be fun. I'll get to see new parts of Minnesota. Maybe find a Dairy Queen along the way. Road trip!

Halfway there on Highway 52-South (I found that DQ in Cannon Falls) the scenery began to change. What had been flat highway morphed into long-sloping hills. Exit signs pointed to towns with names a Scrabble player would love: Wanamingo, Zumbrota, Mazeppa, Oronoco. I recognized Rochester, a rurban metropolis of mini-skyscrapers and hotels encircling the Mayo Clinic, but a few miles further south as we crossed Interstate 90 (east to La Crosse, west to Austin) nothing looked familiar.

It sure looked pretty, though. At Marion Township where the highway squeezes into two lanes, small hills got hillier, curves got curvier. The landscape was dotted with small, tidy farms and thick patches of forest. Coming around one bend we saw people unloading canoes, giving us our first glimpse of the Root River.

Many of the farms we passed were perched on high-terraced hills. The honey-gold and green crops laid out across them looked like Paul Bunyan-sized patchwork quilts. Small herds of cows and horses grazed serenely near white farmhouses with large porches. The colors were vibrant. Weathered red barns, rusted windmills, green John Deere tractors, tall blue silos with white caps. It looked like we'd driven into the pages of a glossy feed store calendar.

Lanesboro has an average of 184 sunny days each year.

Twenty-two miles from Rochester we arrived in Chatfield (Population 2,787) where a banner draped over its main street announced the town's "Western Days" festival. Fifteen minutes later, after more hills and farms, we arrived at Fountain (Population 413) where we turned left on County Road 8. The town sign, proudly proclaiming Fountain as the "Sinkhole Capital of the U.S.A.," seemed a bit jarring in such a small-scale place with a white-steepled Lutheran church, a handful of storefronts ("Where Good Friends Meat," said the sign above Willie's Market), a post office, a bank and a café.

The town was small; above us the sky was big and brilliant blue. Massive white clouds circled the horizon like snow-capped mountains. Outside of Fountain we could see for hundreds of miles in every direction—southeastern Minnesota, western Wisconsin and northern Iowa all at once. I twisted circles in my driver's seat trying to take it all in. Around another curve we passed a man sitting in a chair by the side of the road. I slowed, thinking he might need help. Then I realized he was sitting at an easel, paint brush in hand. He was trying to take it all in, too.

Eight miles later a weathered redwood sign at the crest of another hill announced our destination: "Historic Downtown Lanesboro Welcome." Easing down the steepest grade of the entire trip, we glanced left and had our first look at the town. It was a moment—I will hear so many people say these same words—that I will never forget.

Before us sat a little village in a cozy valley circled by high hills. A high ridge ran through the town center, topped by two church steeples and a water tower. The Root River flows into and around the town, forming its northwest edge. Two large bridges sit above the river, the larger one with metal girders and redwood timbers, the smaller one, built in 1893, is a walking bridge with a dainty, almost Victorian feel. The entire scene had the look of a model railroad diorama, or as a friend later described it, a 3-D pop-up card. Pick your image, it all just fits. Lanesboro was pulling me in. It still does, every time I come down that hill.

At the bottom a low cement bridge brought us to Parkway Avenue, the town's one main street, lined on both sides with red-and-cream brick buildings with classic storefronts and awnings. None house familiar franchises, though. Not a McDonalds, Subways or Starbucks in sight. (Local ordinances forbid them, I'd learn). No stop lights, either. "Arriving in Lanesboro is like walking onto a western movie set," someone tells me later. I like that one, too.

Lanesboro was a busy place this summer morning with bicycles everywhere: standard two-wheelers, tandems, a few recumbents, even a covered surrey with a quartet of riders pedaling hard and laughing harder. Many bikers were cutting across Parkway on a diagonal trail, while less than a hundred yards away in the Root River a group of teens floated by in big yellow-and-blue inner tubes. A few couples were enjoying brunch on a restaurant's outside patio high above the river, while others were licking cones from the corner ice cream parlor. Shoppers casually strolled in and out of nearby jewelry, antique and gift shops. It all looked welcoming and relaxed, like a quaint village in a Hallmark movie. But real.

Turning right on Parkway we quickly passed the History Museum, the Sons of Norway Lodge No. 376, and a large Community Center building. Just past that was Sylvan Park, thickly shaded by dozens of mature oak, elm and maple trees. A large, orange playground was in the Park's center, next to a covered gazebo. Two oblong ponds nearby were circled by fishermen baiting hooks and looking hopeful. Across the ponds, pitched at the foot of a high hill, were a half-dozen yellow, blue and green tents like a row of over-sized rainbow mushrooms.

On the park's eastern side was a small ballfield, tennis courts, and camp sites for larger tents, trailers, and RVs. A few families grilled lunch over campfires while kids were tossed Frisbees and played bean bags. There was lots to see around here. And listen to. Canada geese flew overhead honking loudly and next to one of those tents somebody was plinking a banjo. The sound of flowing water puzzled me until I looked back across Parkway and saw a small dam on the Root River. Standing in a swirling pool below its spillway was a fly fisherman wearing hip-high green waders and making lazy, parabolic casts. He looked hopeful, too.

So this is Lanesboro. I'd expected to find a quiet Minnesota farm town. There was so much more. For the first of so many times this little town was surprising me. "It all feels like one big park," I said to Susie. "There's something a bit magical here." I felt that and said that after being here 15 minutes. Later that morning, while casually visiting with a downtown shopkeeper, I mentioned we were taking a look at a local B & B. "You'll be here in six months," he told me with a smile.

After spending the afternoon, neither of us wanted to leave. Turns out, in a way, we never have. We were discovering the "there" of Lanesboro, Minnesota. Yes, Gertrude, you'd love this place.

Root River bridges

Early Lanesboro woke up early every July 4th to the boom of a cannon fired by Civil War veterans.

Lanesboro... Its Past

The Sons of Norway Lodge

In 1876—the nation's bicentennial—Lanesboro's population reached its highest point, approximately 1,600 people.

Lanesboro...Its Past

Today Minnesota's one major metropolis—the Twin Cities of Minneapolis and St. Paul—dominates the state culturally, politically and economically. That wasn't the case 150 years ago. In 1858, the year Minnesota became a state, more people were living in southeastern Minnesota's Fillmore County than in Hennepin County!

Back then Minnesota was on the edge of America's western frontier. The entire country was on the move. Change was rampant. Railroads were boldly pushing boundaries. Waves of settlers and immigrants were arriving daily, eager to carve out new lives in a new land. Farm lands were newly accessible and agriculture was beginning to flourish. Despite the national turmoil of the Civil War, the future of the American west—and the state of Minnesota—looked bright.

That was especially true in southern Minnesota and in the Root River Valley. Many saw this as an area of great potential and opportunity. A visionary few from New York and Massachusetts even identified a certain spot in that valley that they couldn't resist. The rest, as they say, is history. Lanesboro's history.

A fun history it is! It offers a little mystery (who were the first people to call this place home?), colorful characters (including a visit from one of America's first great celebrities), and true-life stories about hard-working people, many born in far-off lands, whose determination and skill left a proud mark still visible today.

Lanesboro's past is filled with tales of grand hotels, lively town celebrations, big fires, more than a few floods, CCC boys, steam engines replaced by bicycles, and an inspired community brave enough to re-invent itself not just once but multiple times. We'll hear those stories, and since, as Scottish writer Thomas Carlyle once said, "history is biography," we'll also meet a few key people who helped make Lanesboro what it is today.

Lanesboro's history is fun. It can also teach and inspire us. It shows us what can happen when a creative, can-do spirit gets planted in a community and is allowed and encouraged to thrive. This town has a past worth discovering. We're standing on tall shoulders. Let's enjoy the view!

The first home in the Brooklyn neighborhood was built in 1874.

You've Entered...the Driftless Zone

Lanesboro's past begins on a prehistoric "island" most people don't know about.

Lanesboro's past starts way back. Back before railroads and bike trails, back even further than Native Americans and immigrant trails. To fully discover this place you need to start with that long-ago past. That can begin to happen on your drive here. Before you park your car, lick an ice cream cone, or pedal ten feet on the bike trail. It's all right there. If you know where to look, that is.

If you arrived here on Highway 52-South from Rochester, just out of Chatfield you started seeing tall hills—bluffs, they're called—on each side of the road. You see similar bluffs when approaching Lanesboro on Highway 250 or County Road 16. There are so many hills like that around here you often hear this part of Minnesota called "bluff country."

Those bluffs are made up mostly of yellowish-gray limestone rock. Early Lanesboro photographs show the bluff cliffs stark, even bare, but today they're densely covered with trees and shrubs. Many of those bluffs are tens of thousands of years old. Some are hundreds of feet high. You'll see sharp peaks and tall towers. A few even have what look like balancing boulders. It's not quite Utah's Arches Natural Park, but still impressive.

On your drive here you might have also noticed deep, hole-like impressions in farm fields, some so large they look like they're swallowing trees. Remember Fountain's claim about "sinkholes?" That's a clue. More on that in a minute.

On the roads to Lanesboro you see tall bluffs, rolling hills, and large, mysterious holes. What don't you see? Lakes. (Fillmore County is one of only a few counties in Minnesota without one). Other than large ponds, the water around here is moving— rivers, streams, creeks, and springs. (A few springs bubble right out of hillsides). There's lots of cold, clear, moving water around here and that has benefits. Trout love it (along with the people who fish for them). Mosquitos don't. No mosquitos? Toto, maybe we're not in Minnesota anymore.

Well, we are and we aren't. You've arrived in an amazing geological region with a topography unique to Minnesota, the Midwest, even the United States. You have

"Karst" gets its name from Slovenia's "Kraus" plateau. "Kraus" in German means "barren land."

entered (cue Mr. Serling)...the Driftless Zone, a big "island" of nearly 16,000 square miles positioned at the convergence of four U.S. states: Minnesota, Wisconsin, Iowa, and Illinois.

Most people have never heard of "the Driftless." Few can describe it. The name comes from something that didn't happen here. A million years ago (give or take a millennium) a gigantic ice sheet covered most of what we know as the American Midwest and Canada. As glacier mountains melted and slid north (the last one about 10,000 years ago) they carved up the landscape, leaving massive holes that formed all those famous Minnesota lakes and deposited enormous piles of "drift"—rocks, sand and gravel—across the land. But glaciers did not cover this region of prehistoric land. No glaciers. No lakes. No covering of drift. Hence, "driftless." That changed everything.

Without "drift," the forces of nature—primarily water and wind over time—were free to do their erosive work on the unprotected limestone, sandstone, and layered shale left behind. Huge torrents of water from melting glaciers surged across the landscape towards what became the Mississippi River basin, carving out the valleys and bluffs that give the "driftless" area its distinctive look. Native Americans considered it "sacred ground." You can see why.

This unique geology has a related scientific name: "karst." Karst, also rare, is formed when subterranean soft rock, dissolved by running water, becomes a winding underground network of caves and caverns. Like Swiss cheese made out of rock. Karst activity produced thousands of deep caves and caverns around here, like the Niagara Cave in Harmony and the Mystery Cave in Forestville State Park near Preston.

Remember those tree-swallowing holes? In karst topography, some caves are very deep; others lie close to the earth's surface. When a cave ceiling near the surface collapses it creates an opening called a "sinkhole." There may be as many as 10,000 sinkholes in Fillmore County and new ones are still being discovered. Over time, trees and shrubs often grow up from the bottom of a sinkhole. That's what we see driving towards Lanesboro from Fountain. No monstrous, Florida-like sinkholes have swallowed local streets or houses—yet. But there are plenty of sinkholes around here. Watch your step.

The last glacier activity of pre-historic Minnesota halted approximately 35 miles west of Lanesboro.

Early farmers who found sinkholes on their land just plowed around them. They also used them as dumping pits for old farm equipment and other refuse, a practice now illegal. Today trained sinkhole searchers still find old relics along with an occasional fossil.

Lanesboro is in the "driftless zone." What does that mean for the people who live here and for its many visitors? Very cool stuff. It means there's amazing geology to explore and appreciate all around this area. It means that on your bike ride you're looking up at prehistoric limestone bluffs. You can fish in crystal-clear streams that produce some of the best trout in the United States. You can enjoy wild flowers that only grow in a karst environment. You can go "birding" in an area that attracts hundreds of species of migratory birds. It means you can hike into caves to see spring-fed, underground waterfalls. On top of those bluffs you can take in panoramic views of rolling hills and horizon-stretching farmlands that give "flyover country" a majesty that takes your breath away.

What it all really means is this. If Lanesboro didn't have a bike trail to ride, a night of theater to enjoy, a river to canoe, a nice restaurant to eat in, a comfy B & B to sleep in, or local art galleries to browse, this would still be an amazing place to visit, live and enjoy. And it is. All because you're in...the Driftless Zone.

Stone cut by the Lanesboro Dam

Cracks in nearby bluffs "breathe in" warm summer air that's cooled underground before being "breathed out" again, creating an environment in which rare plants thrive.

Mystery in a Farmer's Field

Who first lived in the Root River Valley is a question still searching for an answer.

Farmer Newell was working in his field near the confluence of the Root River on a spring day in 1879 when his plow-blade struck a hard object in the dirt. He stooped to investigate and what he found not only startled him but also raised questions about Lanesboro's earliest history that have never been fully answered.

What the farmer found that day was a human skull.

News about that discovery quickly spread to town. Soon a group of men grabbed shovels and hurried back to the farm. They started to dig and quickly unearthed more human bones. Lots of bones. Over the next few days six cartloads of bones were dug up, the remains of an estimated 600 people. Along with those bones they also found artifacts such as knives, tools, and copper spearheads.

Of all the questions those discoveries raised, two were key. Who were all these people? And why were they buried here?

What they'd found on this farm was a burial mound that was hundreds, perhaps even thousands, of years old. Since the 1700's more than 12,000 similar mounds have been discovered across southern Minnesota. The question of who was buried in the mounds led to many theories, some strange (a mysterious "vanished race of giants," a tall tale that even Abraham Lincoln once referenced), to the stranger (aliens from outer space), to the most likely: these bones were the remains of ancient Native Americans.

An early story—possibly coming from members of the Winnebago (Ho-Chunk) tribe who lived near Lanesboro in the late 1800s—said these mounds held remains from an ancient battle between ancestors of the Dakota and the Chippewa tribes. It was said that this large battle took place near the confluence of the Root River's South and North Branches. The Chippewas won that conflict, the Winnebagos (Ho-Chunk) allegedly claimed, and buried their defeated Dakota foes here.

A second version of that story said it was a battle between the Chippewas and the Winnebagos (Ho-Chunk) that had started in Wisconsin, reached the Mississippi River, and culminated in this bloody conflict near Lanesboro. In this version, the Chippewas were again victorious, and the local mounds were the burial site of defeated Winnebago (Ho-Chunk) warriors.

Newer research indicates both stories are most likely false. Few experts now believe that any major Native American battle took place near Lanesboro. Rather, local burial mounds, like the vast majority of mounds in Minnesota, contain the remains of Native American people who lived here many thousands of years ago. Those Native Americans are now identified as mound-builders from the Upper Mississippian culture.

In the 1600's French fur traders arrived in what would become Minnesota. They met ancestors of Native American tribes that we know today as the Dakota and Ojibwe, who were themselves descendants of cultures going back perhaps thousands of years. The Winnebagos (Ho Chunk) had ancestral homes in pre-historic Wisconsin and later moved to what would become southern Minnesota and northern Iowa. It's likely they passed through, perhaps even lived in, the Root River Valley, using the river for food, navigation and trade, and hunted local game animals for food supplies.

The mid-19th century was a time of turmoil and tension between Native Americans and white settlers in this state. A treaty signed between the Dakota and settlers in 1851 opened the door for homesteading in Fillmore County. Those homesteaders soon included immigrant settlers in areas around the north fork of the Root River.

Farther west in Minnesota treaty tensions and conflicts erupted into violent raids and full-scale warfare during the early 1860s known as the Dakota Conflict. Rumors falsely spread that warring Indians were on the move towards Fillmore County. Panic ensued among a few local settlers who packed up and headed east, only to return weeks later. The Conflict ended on December 26, 1862, with the public hanging of 38 Dakota men in Mankato, Minnesota, the largest public execution in U.S. history.

The Dakota Conflict did have a lasting impact on this area. After the hostilities, Native Americans in southern and western Minnesota were forced into reservations. Their removal "opened" even more land for settlers and immigrants. This was happening at a time when western railroads were pushing westward, making it easier for people to travel here. People were dreaming big dreams about new lands and new lives, and one of those dreams would lead to the birth of Lanesboro, Minnesota.

The discovery of a Native American burial mound in a Lanesboro field tells part of a too-easily ignored story in Minnesota history. (Sadly, more than 80% of the state's burial mound sites were eventually looted, disrupted, even destroyed, making

The earliest hunters, explorers and perhaps settlers in the Root River Valley may have been Native Americans of the Sioux, Chippewa and Winnebago (Ho-Chunk) tribes.

the full narrative impossible to capture.) What we can say is that long before people with last names like Scanlan and Habberstad established farms and homes here, Native Americans had lived, fished, hunted, raised families, and buried their dead here. They were the first people to call this hidden, beautiful valley "home." While mysteries remain, they should not be forgotten.

The first white men to visit bluff country were with a U.S. military regiment traveling from Des Moines to present-day Winona in 1835.

Steam Engines 'Round the Bluff

A railroad line built Lanesboro—twice.

In the 1860s, the convergence of two powerful forces in the Root River Valley created the town of Lanesboro. One was natural: the rushing force of the Root River. The other was man-made: the steel rain lines of the Southern Minnesota Railroad (SMRR). Which played the bigger role in town history? In its arrival, and in its departure a century later, nothing had more impact on Lanesboro, the entire surrounding area in fact, than the railroad.

The Southern Minnesota Railroad, originating in La Crosse, Wisconsin, arrived in Rushford, Minnesota on January 1, 1867—but its owners had their sights set further west. New settlements like Chatfield and Preston lobbied hard to get the railroad to come to their towns. But the railroad owners were excited about a specific section of the Root River 18 miles west of Rushford where the river cut a V-shaped channel through limestone bluffs.

Why did this natural channel get their attention? Steam locomotives need water—lots of it. This channel provided easy access to water. The railroad owners

also saw the potential for a dam to be placed at that spot to harness water power. The power that could run mills, create industry, provide jobs, and build a permanent town. For those reasons and more they decided to push their rail lines that direction from Rushford, with a long-term plan for tracks to go northwest on to Fountain.

The decision was the easy part. Making it happen proved much tougher. An early observer said laying railroad track "... through (the) rugged passages and deep cuts (of the Root River Valley) required pluck, fortitude and capital." Thankfully, all three were in ample supply. Crews of workmen and cartloads of lumber and other construction materials soon began heading out of Rushford on primitive trails. Mile by mile they slugged on. By December, 1868, the Southern Minnesota Railroad line had reached Lanesboro.

Train traffic energized the new community. People and supplies began arriving almost daily, new construction projects sprang up, and local farmers were able to transport their goods to distant markets. Lanesboro was now the western terminus of the SMRR line. Crews even placed a turntable to make rail traffic more efficient.

The railroad went through a number of ownership and name changes. The "Southern Minnesota Railroad Company" became the "Root River Valley and Southern Minnesota Railroad Company." By 1880 the entire operation was absorbed into the famous "Chicago, Milwaukee and St. Paul Railroad Company," most commonly referred to as "The Milwaukee Road."

Over the next decade train traffic increased and the town grew. It was in the late 1870s when the first major difficulties emerged. Crop failures caused by an agricultural disease called wheat smut hurt local farmers, and the "Long Depression" of 1873-1879 (when national unemployment reached nearly 14% and more than 18,000 businesses—including nearly 100 railroads–went bankrupt) hurt everybody. Trains kept running and immigrants were still arriving, but the amount of goods being transported by rail was in decline. Those trends would continue into the early part of the 20th century.

The Great Depression of the 1930s slowed everything even more. Rail traffic declined even further. In coming decades more roads were built across the U.S. and trucks began competing with trains as a way to transport goods. Lanesboro's train

At its peak Lanesboro's railroad had two engine crews, 24-hour service, a turntable and roundhouse, and employed 17 men, and a dozen trains passed through here daily.

traffic noticeably dwindled in the 1940s, 1950s and 1960s. Daily runs disappeared. Sometimes there would be weeks between arriving trains. In 1978 the Milwaukee Road officials sought official permission to close their 50 miles of rail line through the Root River Valley. In June of 1979 that request was granted.

The tearing down of the Lanesboro Depot was the symbolic end of an era. The powerful, huff-puffing of steam engines, the mournful sound of train whistles echoing off the bluffs, and the driving force that had built this town were all gone for good.

The trains were no more, but their tracks remained. Did anyone back then have even the slightest premonition about the role those abandoned lines might play in the next act of Lanesboro history? It's hard to imagine they did, but in many ways, because of those ribbons of steel, Lanesboro's best was yet to come.

Cooks at the Power Plant 1915

A large locomotive called "The Pusher" helped trains get up the steep grade to Fountain. Newer and larger engines made it obsolete after 1918.

A Town is Born

Settlers arrive, homes are built, a dream takes shape.

In the 1850s small groups of settlers began arriving in the Root River Valley, fighting through wilderness to begin new lives. They found land, built primitive homes, started farms, and began raising families. They would also play a vital role in what would soon become a Minnesota boom-town story: the birth of a town called Lanesboro.

John Scanlan, Sr., an immigrant from County Kerry, Ireland, was the area's first permanent white settler. In 1856 he built a log cabin home where he and his wife would raise 10 children. Two years later their homestead became part of the formalized Carroltown Township (named after a signer of the Declaration of Independence) and the new state of Minnesota. Dramatic changes and huge growth were ahead. In 1850 less than 6,100 people lived in Minnesota. By 1900 that total would leap to 1.75 million!

The news that the Southern Minnesota Railroad was moving west towards the Root River Valley caught the attention of a group of entrepreneurs from New York and western Massachusetts. Working with local contacts (including men like Cyrus G. Wykoff, a railroad surveyor) they got excited about the prospect of trains bringing tourists from New York and New England to Minnesota to enjoy a healthy, summer resort community. By early 1868 eleven investors formed the Lanesboro Townsite Company. Twenty-five shares in the Company were quickly purchased at $3,000 each (about $50,000 in today's dollars), and providing working capital to start building a new town.

Why did they choose the name "Lanesboro?" Two theories persist. One is a possible connection between Company investors and Lanesborough, Massachusetts, a small town in the Berkshire Mountains. (The fact that the first Post Office here used that spelling adds weight to that theory). A second is that the town was named in honor of F.A. Lane, one of the first investors. Perhaps there's a bit of truth in both.

The Company moved quickly and purchased 500 acres of land from settlers and farmers, including the Scanlans, at $30 an acre. On July 4, 1868, a handful of investors and agents arrived to meet with local businessmen and start work. A platt

In May, 1858, Carrolton Township had approximately 250 inhabitants.

for the town was finalized and three priority construction projects were identified: a road off the north bluff to improve town access, a dam on the Root River to harness water power, and a high-quality hotel for tourists and travelers.

Thomas W. Brayton from New York was chosen as the overall project supervisor. Enthusiasm ran high, work started immediately, and the progress they made was nothing short of remarkable. In December, 1868, the Southern Minnesota Railroad

Coffee Street 1890's

line arrived in town. Despite wilderness conditions and Minnesota winters, the north bluff road was completed, the dam was constructed, and the hotel was in place all within two years. In 1869 Lanesboro was incorporated as a full-fledged Minnesota town. It's impossible to imagine a similar scenario happening today.

New homes were built, businesses started (including W.H. Robert's New York Store boasting 20,000 items of dry goods and groceries), hotels (like the Grant and the American) were doing good business, and more people—including many European immigrants—began moving here. Mills went up powered by the new dam. Local newspapers started. Agriculture grew into an early and enduring foundation of the local economy, with local farmers growing wheat, corn, even a little tobacco. Lumber was important. So was the arrival of those anticipated tourists. Banks were started, goods were being delivered and purchased. A little bluff country town had been born with great promise for days ahead.

The Lanesboro Herald published its first edition in September, 1868.

Michael Scanlan

"Security, Good Service and a Square Deal to All"
Scanlan-Habberstad Bank Motto

Michael Scanlan was born in 1840 in County Kerry, Ireland. He came to this country with his parents when he was 14. The Scanlans first settled in Ohio but Michael and his brother, Cornelius, continued on to Minnesota. (One account tells of them walking from Brownsville in Houston County to Preston, a distance of nearly sixty miles.) Michael's parents soon followed their sons to Minnesota and established a homestead in the Carrolton Township.

While working on his father's farm, young Michael began showing signs of the leadership skills that would set the course of his life. He was elected township clerk at age 19, a position he'd hold for the next 40 years. He started a hardware store, later sold real estate (including some of his own land to the Lanesboro Townsite Company), and was elected to the Minnesota House in 1869.

Banking would be Michael Scanlan's greatest career achievement. He started his own bank in 1880 and in partnership with O.M. Habberstad, he expanded it in 1897. The Scanlan-Habberstad bank would become the largest bank in Fillmore County. At one point fraudulent banking activities in Minneapolis cost his bank more than $20,000. Scanlan assumed those liabilities personally and eventually paid off every one of his depositors in full. He remained the bank's president until his death in 1922 at age 82.

Michael Scanlan left an unequalled reputation in Lanesboro for honesty, integrity and community service. Levang's Weekly, the official Lanesboro newspaper of those years, wrote this about him in 1919: "What Lanesboro is today—one of the livest and most prosperous towns in the state—is probably as due to him with his unflinching faith in its future and his never-flagging efforts in building it up—as to any other living man."

John Scanlan Sr. from Ireland, the area's first settler, passed away in 1889 at the age of 92.

Lanesboro's Stone Dam

Part engineering marvel, part power-driving generator, part inspiring work of art,
the Lanesboro Dam has stood with stability and style for 150 years.

Lanesboro's Stone Dam is located on the Root River just across from the school. As tall as a three-story building and half a football field in length, it's larger than it appears from a distance. It's not imposing, though. Like the town itself, the Dam, completed in 1868, fits its spot so perfectly you can't imagine it not being there.

The bold idea to construct a dam to harness the power of the Root River pre-dates Lanesboro. The owners of the Southern Minnesota Railroad recognized the potential for such a dam when they made the decision to head this way from Rushford. The Lanesboro Townsite Company had a dam on their list of three essentials for the new town, and construction began soon after company agents first arrived.

Colonel W.H. Walford from Rushford supervised the project. A man named Porter was its chief engineer. But it was a group of skilled stonemasons, many of them Scandinavian immigrants with names like Erickson, Nelson, Benson, Enger and Olson, who were the stone masons who put this dam in place. Working with 19th century tools and moving tons of limestone and other rock, they accomplished this mind-boggling construction feat for less than $15,000 (about $250,000 in 2017 dollars).

The dam didn't pause the river without a little drama, though. A few weeks along work was progressing well until one day when, according to one shaken eyewitness, the dam suddenly collapsed with "...a mighty crash...followed immediately by a wall of water twenty feet high (striking) the bridge (and sending) timbers flying in the most terrifying manner possible." A few nearby homes and buildings were flooded; thankfully no lives were lost. Determined crews quickly returned to work and before long construction was completed. While showing signs of age, that same Dam has remained strong and stable ever since.

The Lanesboro Dam's most impressive feature is something you can't even see— how it was put together. The dam is made of individual, two-foot thick limestone blocks hand-carved out of nearby bluffs. Amazingly, no cement or mortar holds them together. Each level of stone was positioned like the steps to a house, several

The Lanesboro Dam is on the South Branch of the Root River. It will be 150 years old in 2018.

inches back from the front of the one below it. Strategically-balanced like a Lego tower, the force of the Root River holds the entire structure in place.

Once completed, the Dam had immediate impact on the new town. A small group of mills sprouted on what was then called Mill Pond (today's Bass Pond) to take advantage of the surging water power. One proud mill owner, James A. Thompson, built his impressive red-brick Italianate home on a hill just south of the dam. (It is the Thompson House Bed & Breakfast today). Those early mills helped local farmers and provided jobs, and despite a number of fires and rebuilds, remained in operation for the next thirty years.

The Lanesboro Stone Dam

Another benefit of the Dam delighted both tourists and residents: a 400-acre recreational lake formed behind it! Two miles long, a mile wide, and as deep as 35 feet, Mill Pond Lake offered warm weather delights for boaters, swimmers and fisherman. In winter it was a popular ice-skating spot. The lake's fun proved short-lived, however, when heavy river silt and local karst topography caused it to fill in just a few years later. Sometimes called Lost Lake, it's located in memory only at the site of the present-day Lanesboro High School football field. During times of heavy rain and occasional flooding, though, the lake makes a bit of an encore.

An additional benefit of the Dam presented itself three decades after it was built when local resident Ed Lynch proposed using its water power to provide electricity. Lynch optimistically claimed the Dam could generate enough hydro-electric power

A lake formed behind the Lanesboro Dam that was two miles long, a mile wide, and up to 35 feet deep. After it silted in and disappeared it was called "Lost Lake" and the land became a state game refuge, and later, a high school football field.

for the energy needs of 15,000 people. People liked his ideas, generators were built, and a small power plant was soon constructed on the site of an abandoned mill that had burned. Lynch personally wired homes and businesses and served as the plant's first supervisor, living in the small brick building that—with later modifications— still stands today next to the Bass Pond.

Lanesboro's power plant never fully reached Lynch's projections, but it did provide electricity—and still does! The Lanesboro Dam is one of the oldest still-functioning hydro-electric dams in the United States. (Only six like it are thought to remain). In 2016, the Lanesboro Dam broke a record by producing more than 1.1 million kilowatts of power. That translates into green, sustainable energy that saved Lanesboro residents more than $70,000 on their electric bills. Not bad for an antique!

A visit to Lanesboro isn't complete without a close-up view of the Stone Dam. On quiet summer days you'll find water flowing peacefully over a spillway and people fishing below it. You might even see trout leaping salmon-like out of the river against the current. Tubers launch their river rides here, kids splash on its small, sandy beach. You'll feel the river's mist and hear its strong, but soothing rush. On days like that, people love taking wedding and graduation pictures here.

After early spring snow melt or a heavy March rain, it's a much different scene. On those days the Root River can be loud, fierce, roaring even, as torrents of water explode over the spillway and down the sloped hillsides on each side. Fun to see. Not something you want to get close to.

As we mentioned, there are wrinkles of age on Lanesboro's dam. Each year more water leaks through spaces between its limestone blocks. In 2017, after years of debate, the Minnesota State Legislature approved $4-million for major dam repairs. Work is scheduled to begin in the late fall of 2018.

That makes many people happy. The Lanesboro Stone Dam is a state historical treasure, a monument to pioneer vision and craftsmanship, and a still-functioning provider of clean, sustainable power. Most of all, the Lanesboro Dam stands strong as the symbolic heart of a little town that probably wouldn't be here without it.

Lanesboro's power plant provided electricity to homes and businesses by the mid-1890s but shut down daily at 1 a.m.

Thomas W. Brayton

The man in charge of building a town.

Thomas W. Brayton of New York was one of the first agents of the Lanesboro Townsite Company. He came to the Root River Valley in 1868 at their request. In a testament to his vision and leadership skills, Brayton was soon designated the "man in charge," the general supervisor given the task to get this town built.

The local paper described him as "...a Christian gentleman of sound judgement and winning ways." He was enthusiastic about the town's potential and was an early proponent of building mills that could use the water power generated by the Lanesboro Dam.

Brayton's vision for Lanesboro's economic potential stirred debate, even some controversy. He encouraged local farmers to plant cotton that could be processed into cloth. Such an enterprise, Brayton lobbied, could easily support a town of at least 1,500 people.

Sadly, Brayton's ideas were never tested because he passed away just a few years after coming to Lanesboro. Mills did get built but they produced grain and flour. Despite how that story ended, Thomas W. Brayton can and should be remembered for helping guide Lanesboro's early construction as one of the great boom-town stories in Minnesota history.

A Post Office opened here in November, 1868, first using the name (and spelling) of "Lanesborough."

34

Lanesboro's Grand Hotel

Its name was eerily but only partially prophetic.

By 1869 the Lanesboro Townsite Company was making impressive progress on its three construction priorities. The Root River had a dam. The north bluff had a road. And that temporary rail line running from a nearby bluff to the center of town was a sign that the Company's third essential would soon be complete as well—a luxury hotel.

Located on what's now Coffee Street near the present Little River General Store, this hotel would become a five-star attraction for its time. Its Grand Opening in 1870 was celebrated with a lavish public meal that cost its owners more than $2,000 ($35,000 in 2017 dollars) and was one of Lanesboro's first big, city-wide celebrations. Sometimes referred to as "The Lanesboro Hotel" and "The Stone Hotel," this was the Phoenix Hotel.

Early Lanesboro had hotels serving travelers and tourists, but the Phoenix Hotel raised local accommodations to a new level of opulence. It became exactly what the founders had hoped—a luxury hotel that helped put Lanesboro on the map and made this little town, for the first but certainly not the last time, a destination.

The building was designed by a William Listman, a German immigrant who later built churches and the court house in La Crosse, Wisconsin. The Phoenix cost $50,000 to build (nearly $1-million in today's dollars), was four stories tall including a walk-out basement level, and had spacious guest rooms with the finest of furnishings, such as imported crystal chandeliers, red plush furniture, marble top dressers, and dark oak woodwork. It was one of the first hotels west of the Mississippi to have steam heat. Many of its rooms had their own fireplaces.

The hotel quickly became the center of town life, home to not just the railroad depot but a popular saloon as well. There was no better place in town to catch up on far-off news and a little local gossip, too. It also had first-floor office space that housed a variety of businesses, including a law office and the medical clinic (a "sanitarium," he called it) of Dr. Frank (White Beaver) Powell, town doctor and celebrated friend of

The Phoenix Hotel—located on Coffee Street—went up in the middle of what was then a wheat field.

William (Buffalo Bill) Cody. Long before the term "medical destination center" was in local vogue (thanks to the Mayo Clinic in nearby Rochester), the Phoenix Hotel in Lanesboro was attracting people here for good doctoring and healthy living, due in large part due to the advertising skills of Dr. Powell. (We'll hear more about him later).

The Phoenix was quickly hailed as the finest hotel in southern Minnesota, perhaps in all the Midwest. (One reviewer even compared it to the finest hotels between Chicago and San Francisco). Its landlords—C.L. Chase and H.H. White—were justifiably proud and optimistic about the future of their business. For the next 15 years the Phoenix Hotel stood tall in the town's center, the hub of a busy—even booming—new community.

All that suddenly and sadly changed on Sunday, May 3, 1885. At 12:35 a.m., flames were spotted in a lower floor of the Phoenix. A major fire erupted (the cause was never confirmed although some blamed a discarded cigar in the hotel's back alley) and despite valiant attempts by local volunteers the entire building was destroyed. Clean-up crews managed to salvage a few charred limestone blocks but little else. Considered too costly to rebuild, this phoenix would not rise from any ashes.

Legend says that those salvaged blocks were later used in foundations for new buildings then under construction, including what we know today as the Old Village Hall and the Stone Mill Suites. If true, shadows of early Lanesboro luxury, quality and pride do live on, and so does the glorious memory of Lanesboro's grand Phoenix Hotel.

Steam Engine at the Phoenix Hotel

Dr. Frank (White Beaver) Powell

Western hero, flamboyant doctor, this town has never seen another one like him.

David Frank Powell was born in a log cabin Kentucky in 1847. His father was a Scottish doctor. His mother was part Senecan Indian. Both lines of heritage would play a major role in his life, especially in his time in Lanesboro.

As a boy Powell was drawn to the American west. By the early 1860s he had become an Army scout where he met and befriended another scout—a man whose life he both mirrored and emulated—named William Cody. The future Buffalo Bill.

Both young men shared a love for adventure, a gift for story-telling, and an entrepreneurial vision to share their stories with a wider (paying) public. Their

White Beaver (second row, second left) and friends

"White Beaver. Surgery a specialty. Cross eyes straightened in one minute. Cataract, Bat's Wing, Granulated Lids, Ulcers of the Cornea, and all other diseases of the eye skillfully treated. Deformities remedied by either operations or scientifically applied apparatus." (Lanesboro Leader ad, April 16, 1881)

timing couldn't have been better. Americans in the 1870s, especially those living in the "civilized" east, had big appetites for wild-west adventure stories. Soon Powell and Cody were the stars of dime-store western novels. That was only the beginning, especially for Cody.

Powell returned to Kentucky for more medical training. Around 1877 he arrived in Lanesboro and opened a medical practice that specialized in treatment of "the diseases of the female and of the eyes." His Native American heritage helped him connect with the local Ho-Chunk (Winnebago) tribe. One story tells of Powell helping that tribe survive a smallpox epidemic after which they bestowed upon him the honorary title of "White Beaver." At a time when natural cures were gaining in popularity, Powell eagerly incorporated this honor into his medical "brand." Calling himself a "medicine chief," he advertised remedies such as "White Beaver Cough Crème" that he promised (even guaranteed) would cure diseased lungs.

A trusted doctor, Powell was also a hugely colorful character. Well over six feet tall, he had long black hair, a large mustache, and typically made his medical rounds on horseback wearing full western buckskin. He was an excellent marksman and was able and willing to shoot apples off the heads of brave volunteers. In August, 1877, he was bit by a rattlesnake. His recovery added another notch to his legend.

Around 1877, his old friend Cody, now widely-known as "Buffalo Bill" because of his hunting and cowboy exploits, arrived in Lanesboro to visit his old friend. It's fun to imagine these two bigger-than-life characters strutting down local wooden sidewalks in full western get-up, fishing the Root River, enjoying a beer or two— and telling big stories—in one of the town's lively saloons.

Local legend says the two men also spent time brainstorming ways to transform Cody's adventure stories into an outdoor show featuring cowboys and Indians, sharp-shooters, trick riders, horses and buffalo. Many believe that Cody and Powell even staged a small-scale "dress rehearsal" in Lanesboro for such a show, a production that eventually grew into Buffalo Bill's internationally-famous "Wild West and Congress of Rough Riders of the World."

In 1881 Dr. Powell and his wife, Bertie, moved to La Crosse, Wisconsin, where he continued to practice medicine, became a popular mayor, even ran (unsuccessfully) for governor. While traveling on a train to Los Angeles in May, 1906, he died of a heart attack at the age of 59.

"The climate, atmosphere and surrounds of Lanesboro are particularly suited to in-valids. That is why I make this place my headquarters." Dr. Frank (White Beaver) Powell

Immigrant Trails

"Go west, young man!"

Horace Greeley

When New York journalist and politician Horace Greely proclaimed that famous advice in 1865, lots of people were listening. Over the next quarter-century America's western frontier was flooded with a tidal wave of settlers, pioneers, farmers, ranchers, gold miners, visionaries, and immigrants. This massive people-movement across the U.S. changed everything in this country—including a little town called Lanesboro.

The lands that became the territory and eventually the state of Minnesota had been home to Native Americans for thousands of years. In the 17th century explorers and fur trappers arrived, soon followed by pioneers and lumbermen eager to make their way in this wilderness. Minnesota joined the Union in 1858. Railroads continued to push west and lands were opening for people seeking new homes. None were more eager than tens of thousands of European immigrants sadly forced to leave their homelands.

People in countries like Ireland, Germany, Norway, and Sweden suffered greatly during the mid- and latter part of the 19th century. Food shortages and famines, economic upheaval, unemployment, farm foreclosures, political instability, over-crowding, epidemics, and religious conflicts made life challenging, if not unbearable. Those conditions forced thousands of families to make the life-wrenching decision to uproot their lives and find other places to live. Many looked to America for hope of that better life.

Many of them chose Minnesota as their destination. By the 1890's the foreign-born population of the U.S. was approximately 15%. In Minnesota it was nearly 40%. In the 1896 election Minnesota voter instructions were offered in nine languages: English, German, Norwegian, Swedish, Finnish, French, Czech, Italian, and Polish. Diversity was a way of life in Minnesota from its earliest days.

By the 1870s Lanesboro's train depot was welcoming a daily influx of immigrants, especially from Germany, Norway, Sweden and Ireland. While some used

The North Bluff area of Lanesboro was also known as Irish Ridge.

rail lines to leap-frog further west, many decided to stay here. On more than a few occasions husbands who temporarily settled their wives and children here while searching for land ended up returning to Lanesboro because their wives refused to leave!

They liked it here for many reasons. Available farmland was a plus. Its strong Scandinavian culture was comfortable to many. It was a time of opportunity, growth and hopeful promise, all plusses to people who had recently faced so many difficulties.

Many early immigrants also came to America from Ireland during that country's potato famine from 1845-1852. The majority of Irish immigrants remained in the northeast U.S., but some did come as far west as the Minnesota territory, arriving in communities like Olmsted, Wabasha and Winona. A handful of Irish families also settled near the Mississippi River in southeastern Minnesota, including the Scanlan family (as we learned earlier) who came to the Root River Valley in the 1850s and helped found Lanesboro.

Many immigrants ended up here from Norway for some obvious reasons. Nearly 80% of Norwegian immigrants arriving in the U.S. in the latter half of the 19th century had left farm and rural backgrounds in the old country. Midwest farm land offered a life familiar to them. Many had first settled in Wisconsin but by the 1850s land there was getting scarce. So they headed further west to Minnesota, to towns like Spring Grove (where "Norwegian Ridge" became the cultural center of early Norwegian life in the United States) and Lanesboro. By the early 1900s, when immigrant waves peaked locally and state-wide, Lanesboro had become predominantly Norwegian.

Early Lanesboro School

The Norwegians brought with them a strong work ethic, farming experience, craftsmanship (the Lanesboro Dam is a superb example), dedication to faith (small but classic Lutheran churches are strewn throughout bluff country), and strong family ties. Lanesboro's Lutheran Church was a prominent structure on Church

Hill by the 1870s, the Sons of Norway fraternal organization was established in 1929, and even in the 1930s and beyond it was still common to hear Norwegian spoken on city streets.

Those early Norwegian roots were planted deep. Minnesota is still home to more Norwegians than any other state, and Norwegian life and culture remain evident and respected in Lanesboro. You find that in the Commonweal Theatre's long-running (and internationally-recognized) Ibsen Festival that spotlighted the plays of Henrik Ibsen's, Norway's eminent writer and the "father of the modern play." Norwegian meatballs are always on the menu of the Pedal Pusher Café, and lefse is a staple at town festivals and the Parkway Market.

Many German immigrants also arrived in southern Minnesota, including Lanesboro, during the late 1800s. (Historians point to Edward Pelz, an expatriate who fled Germany and came to Minnesota for influencing many Germans to move to this state). German immigrants helped establish towns like New Ulm, St. Cloud and Shakopee. By 1905 there were actually more Germans in Minnesota than Scandinavians. Today there are more people of German ancestry in the state than any other ethnic background. St. Patrick's Catholic Church in Lanesboro became a spiritual and cultural home for many local Germans.

By the 1890s the majority of Minnesota farmlands had been claimed. Fewer immigrants were arriving. By the mid-1930s the combination of national quotas, the Great Depression and World War II slowed their numbers even more. What had been a century of cultural turmoil began to settle, at least for a period of time. The immigrants who helped establish this community became part of a tapestry still visible, respected and celebrated today.

Norwegian remained the language spoken at Sons of Norway meetings until 1949.

William (Buffalo Bill) Cody

The Showman comes to town.

Lanesboro's biggest holiday is held on the first weekend in August and features live music, family barbecues, softball and volleyball tournaments, a street dance, fireworks, and a Sunday parade. Why the big party? One clue used to be the lady riding a buffalo in that parade. This is Buffalo Bill Days!

Buffalo Bill (seated left) and Dr. Powell (seated right)

William Cody, born in Le Claire, Iowa, in 1846, was the most famous American on the planet in the late 1800s. Like Forrest Gump, he showed up everywhere. He was a Pony Express rider at age 14, an Army scout, a famous buffalo hunter, and a decorated Civil War soldier. He acted in New York, lunched with the Pope, had tea with Queen Victoria, and rode horses with Theodore Roosevelt. When France dedicated the Eiffel Tower on March 31, 1889, Buffalo Bill was an honored guest. One of the great entertainers of his generation, Cody created and took his wild west show—part-rodeo, part-carnival, part live-action history theater—on a thirty-year world tour seen by more than 70 million people.

As we learned earlier, Buffalo Bill came to Lanesboro in the late 1870s to visit his long-time friend, Dr. Frank (White Beaver) Powell. Some believe the two men

A bluff east of Lanesboro is known as "Buffalo Bill's Peak."

planned Buffalo Bill's earliest shows here. People in Nebraska disagree claiming that Cody's first "real" show took place in Omaha in 1883. Like many Buffalo Bill stories, the exact truth may never be known. It is true, though, that he was here and Lanesboro enthusiastically celebrates that fact every August.

There's another possible Lanesboro angle to all this. In the 1870s, during the same time period he was visiting Lanesboro, Cody passed through scenic countryside near Yellowstone National Park in Wyoming. It's reported that he was impressed with that area's potential. A new railroad was bringing people there. Good farm land was available. Hunting was plentiful. Did all of that remind Buffalo Bill of Lanesboro? We know he soon talked about planning a town. In the 1890s he returned to Wyoming and did just that, and Cody, Wyoming, incorporated in 1901, is still flourishing today. Are Lanesboro, Minnesota and Cody, Wyoming twin towns separated at birth, or is this just one more Buffalo Bill story? We'll never know for sure.

Buffalo Bill's Peak

Let's Move the River!

Lanesboro's can-do spirit makes an early appearance.

Lanesboro is a river town. The Root River brought the railroad here. The river powered its first mills and created jobs that helped start the town. The river made transportation easier. It even became a source of local electric power. Jump ahead 150 years and you see the Root River re-energizing Lanesboro through "tourist power," with people coming here to tube, kayak, canoe and fish.

Yes, the Root River has been great for Lanesboro. But over the years the river also created a few problems. Flooding is an obvious one. Residents here keep a careful eye on the river during big storms and spring thaws. Floods, mostly minor, a few major, are a fact of life in a river town like this one.

The major problem with the Root River in early Lanesboro was its location. This moderate-sized river twists, turns and winds its way through a narrow valley. In the town's earliest history, the river flowed differently than it does today. It actually wound its way through Sylvan Park. When the Lanesboro Townsite Company platted the town those bends presented a number of challenges, and they learned quickly that the Root was a river with a mind of its own.

The big problem was transportation. Getting from Point A to Point B in Lanesboro was a daily ordeal, especially if you lived "south" in the neighborhood known then as now known as Brooklyn. The river left those houses with no direct downtown access. Walks were long, cart travel was slow, moving goods was especially difficult. A few smaller bridges helped but didn't solve the problem.

How that problem finally did get solved is an early example of Lanesboro's creative, can-do spirit. People knew the river's location created problems so a cry went up—"let's move the river!" In 1874, that's exactly what they did.

Careful planning and lots of hard work accomplished a giant task. Primitive earth-moving equipment supplemented many strong backs and shovels as they diverted the water to remove the river's serpentine bend through Sylvan Park. They guided the river to a new course parallel to what is now called Parkway Avenue.

The Root River flows through the driftless region for about 80 miles.

Moving the river didn't eliminate all flooding problems. Time would prove that. But it did make travel much easier for town locals. Later modifications improved transportation even more and eased the risks of seasonal flooding.

The Root River can still be a bit stubborn. Signs of its original course—most notably the two spring-fed ponds in Sylvan Park that flow into a small creek by the Sons of Norway Lodge—are still visible today. After heavy rains water pools in the parking lot behind the Lanesboro School. Some say it isn't just the rain coming down that creates that problem, it's the underground water tables (the original river?) coming up to the surface. A river that loves an encore.

Root River Bridge

Robert R. Greer, originally from Canada, became Lanesboro's first mayor in 1868.

Olaf M. Habberstad

From store clerk to bank president, another immigrant makes his mark.

Olaf M. Habberstad was born in Norway in 1866. At the age of four he sailed with his parents to America on a harrowing trip that took 13 weeks. His family, like many Norwegian immigrants of that period, made their way to southeastern Minnesota and to Lanesboro. Olaf was one of nine siblings, a number of whom left a positive mark on this town for decades to come.

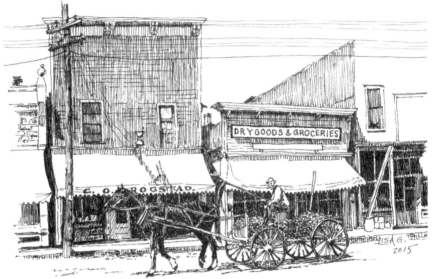

Hauling fertilizer down main street

In 1897 Michael Scanlan wanted to expand his banking business, so he approached Olaf, then 31, who had once worked for him as a store clerk. The two formed a partnership that grew into the Scanlan-Habberstad Bank & Trust Company, one of the dominant economic institutions in Fillmore County.

O.M. eventually became president of that bank, as well as Lanesboro town treasurer, president of the Kiwanis Club, and a member of the Odd Fellows service club. He also helped develop Sylvan Park. The elegant Victorian home he built on Fillmore Ave. S. later became a hospital, and today is the beautiful Habberstad House Bed & Breakfast.

The Lanesboro Band played for iceskaters waltzing on Mill Pond in the late 1870s

Leather Lungs on Ski Jump Hill

"On a clear, cold day, you could hear his voice for miles!"

Take a short drive north out of Lanesboro on Highway 250 and you'll find rolling farmlands and sloping hills. It won't immediately grab your attention, but one of those hills put this little town on the national, even international, sports map about a century ago. Seriously.

In the early 1920s R.O. Benson had a farm in that area. He also had six sons. In the long, cold Minnesota winters, R.O. needed to find something to keep his sons busy. Benson looked at his tall hill and had an idea. A very Norwegian idea.

Norwegians and skiing go back centuries. By 1800 that included skiing down high hills and jumping off to see how far you could go. Soon people were competing at it and its popularity spread across Europe and even to North America. It became an official Winter Olympics event in 1924. It's not a sport for the faint-hearted (the famous opening scenes of ABC's "Wide World of Sports" featured a bouncing Olympic ski-jumper symbolizing "the agony of defeat"), but ski-jumping remains popular around the world.

Back to Benson's hill. After clearing trees and brush, the father and his boys created the first—many say the best—long-jump hill in southern Minnesota. The Benson ski area and its 175-feet long hill soon became a popular venue for recreational skiing and ski-jump tournaments for at least a decade. In the 1920s, crowds of more than 2,000 spectators traveled icy back roads to Lanesboro for annual tournaments to watch some of the best long-jumpers in the U.S. and the world compete for awards sanctioned by the National Ski Association.

Two Olafs from Lanesboro became famous on that hill. Olaf Evenson was the best local ski jumper and took home many trophies. Olaf Thompson of the Thompson Brothers Furniture Store became a nationally-recognized ski-jump race announcer. His booming voice, enhanced with his large megaphone, gave him the nickname

"There's not a better town of its size in the Northwest than Lanesboro...(It) has the finest water power on the Root River, building stones in unlimited quantities, good water, picturesque scenery, everything to make this one of the most thriving cities in Minnesota. " (Hartford, Connecticut Journal and Courier, 1889.)

"Leather Lungs." Thompson called hundreds of ski jump competitions at Benson Hill in Lanesboro, in Minnesota, and even across the country.

Times and interests change. Within a few years Lanesboro's annual ski jump competitions ended and the local hill was abandoned. (Not before one local lad allegedly took his sled down it with bumpy and near disastrous results). You can drive by the hill today, though, and try to imagine how all that looked and sounded ("listen, there's Leather Lungs!") a century ago when Lanesboro, Minnesota, for a fleeting moment, was one of the ski jump capitals of the world.

Ski jump at Benson Hill 1920s

The Park School House, built in 1882, was swept away in a flood eight years later.

G.B. Ellestad

Lanesboro's hometown Edison

Gilbert B. Ellestad was born near Mabel, Minnesota, in 1859, yet another son of Norwegian immigrants. As a little boy Gilbert loved fixing mechanical things. He would take apart family clocks and his mother's sewing machine just to put them back together. In his teens he'd walk for miles to nearby farms, offering his services as a repairman and building a reputation for excellent skills and good service.

Gilbert made his way to Chicago in his early 20s (it was said he walked most of the way there, too) for training in watch-making and repair. By 1890 he returned to Lanesboro where he opened his own watch, jewelry and gift store. (His local ad promised "...a large assortment of chains, charms, lockets, silverware and spectacles, and good, reliable time keepers in nickel cases from $4-$10.") He married, had three sons, served as Lanesboro mayor for nearly a decade, and lived the life of a respected and successful businessman.

And a tinkerer. In the mold of a contemporary, the famous American inventor Thomas Edison, G.B. Ellestad had a creative and inventive mind. Like Edison, he also had a special interest in electricity. He used wires, magnets, and old cracker boxes to craft two telephones and installed a line from his downtown shop to his Brooklyn neighborhood home. It was the first private phone line in town and was still usable 20 years later. He invented an alarm system for his jewelry store and an automatic timer that turned off his shop's kerosene lamp the same time each evening. He and his sons, Gerhard and Irwin, installed a wireless telegraph system in their home's basement on which they communicated with telegraph operators 30 miles away in Iowa. Time-keeping always fascinated him. In 1912 he ran a wire from nearby bluffs to his shop that allowed him to receive the exact time daily from the National Aeronautics Association station in Arlington, Virginia.

The Ellestad boys—with free time and a little electricity—were known to playfully sidetrack their dad's inventive ways. When a neighbor's chickens disrupted tomatoes in the Ellestad garden, the boys wired one of their father's induction coils to a metal pan and baited it with corn. Soon the squawk of shocked chickens filled the back

Some records show you could open a saloon in Lanesboro in the 1880s with a $15 license—there may have been as many as a dozen in town.

yard and the trespassing birds scurried home. An electrified "hot seat" in an outhouse on a Lanesboro farm was also traced to the Ellestad boys. Raising it a notch, the boys devised "magic lantern shows" in their Brooklyn basement (admission: one penny) that offered some of the first "picture shows" in town history.

By the early 2000s, the Ellestad watch and gift shop was long gone. But in the same building where his store had been, a new restaurant opened and honored him by calling itself "Gil B's." This good, curious and talented tinkerer would once again have a presence on main street of the town he loved.

G.B. Ellestad's Jewelry Store

Dr. Frank (White Beaver) Powell's two brothers—William (Bronco Bill) and George (Night Hawk)—also lived here in the 1870s.

Fires, Floods and Mayhem

It's not the crisis—but how you handle it—that matters.

A leisurely stroll in downtown Lanesboro on a late summer afternoon defines serenity. Sweet light casts shadows on nearby bluffs. Red, yellow and blue wildflowers spill from antique lamp posts. Behind vintage store fronts, the Root River ripples peacefully under the trusses of an abandoned railroad bridge. Monet would have something to work with here. It's easy to think of the entire town as an oasis far removed from any upheaval, drama or strife.

Well, think again.

That's not to say this little village hides a dark nature or that what you're seeing and feeling isn't real. Lanesboro is most often peaceful and serene. It's also true that this town has been battered by its share of natural calamities. (A few man-made ones,

In October, 1885 children playing with matches set R.R. Greer's barn on fire. Greer's three-year-old son lost his life in that blaze.

too. Did you hear about the love-sick police chief who took the term "flame" way too literally? We'll get to that). What would history be—including Lanesboro's—without a few fires, floods and general mayhem?

Let's start with the natural ones. Lanesboro sits in the southeast corner of one of the most weather-turbulent states in the country. Minnesota's violent summer storms, monstrous snow dumps, spring floods, ripping high winds, and major-league tornadoes can happen—or at least threaten—here. And they leave a mark.

Floods, for instance. This small town, wedged into a narrow valley between high bluffs, also has a robust river running through it. Floods became a fact of life here. We talked earlier about one of the first floods that happened in 1868 when the Lanesboro Dam gave way early in its construction. Less than a decade later, in the "Great Flood" of March 10, 1876, the Root River surged over its banks. (A tragic story from that event pictures the human toll: the day before the flood, Dennis Galligan's 11-year-old daughter had drowned. When waters rose on the 10th, her family ran for safety, able to carry only a few personal items—and the body of their deceased child.) Another flood hit town in January, 1894, a rare winter flood. The Park School House, built in 1882 near Sylvan Park, was flooded many times before being totally swept off its foundation in 1890. Black-and-white photographs of a major flood in Lanesboro on August 13, 1911 show so much water rushing over the Lanesboro Dam that the Dam itself is nearly obliterated.

The Flat, Lanesboro's eastern-most section, is the town's most vulnerable flood area, due to its low terrain and proximity to the river. That was true most recently in the August of 2007 when a major storm dumped 17 inches of rain in Fillmore County, most of that near Rushford, but Lanesboro felt effects, too. Heavy rains can bring flooding. They can also create landslides. The North Bluff Landslide in the winter of 1904 resulted in teams of horses being used to move a bridge nearly 500 feet across ice and snow.

Floods are frightening. Fires can be terrifying. Lanesboro's earliest structures, mostly made of wood and heated by woodstoves and coal furnaces, were especially vulnerable to fires. Many buildings, especially on Church Hill, have also caught on fire after lightning strikes.

In early Lanesboro the Village Hall bell was rung nightly at 10 p.m. to signal town curfew.

The town's early mills produced flour. The milling process also produced highly combustible flour dust. In September, 1876, the Thompson & Williams Mill was the first Lanesboro mill to burn down. Rebuilt as the Remington & Leahy Mill, it was leveled by fire again sixteen years later. The Nash & Gilbert Mill burned in 1887. The White & Benyon Mill, the last of the three original mills on Mill Pond, went up in flames in 1902. That was rebuilt, but burned again in 1934. Apparently everyone had had enough and given the additional challenges of the Great Depression, it wasn't replaced.

Fires have damaged major town landmarks throughout its history. We heard earlier about the Phoenix Hotel burning down in May, 1885. On February 23, 1917, lightning on Church Hill ignited a major blaze that destroyed the Old Stone School, the Lutheran Church, and the Lanesboro School. (Only St. Patrick's Catholic Church escaped the conflagration). The Lutheran church was quickly rebuilt and a new school building was in place for the next school year. Sadly another fire struck the top floor of the school on August 5, 1919. Repaired and rebuilt, the building continued to operate as a school until the early 1990s.

The popular White Front Café on the north end of Parkway Ave. was one of three buildings gutted by fire on July 5, 1940. (The Café was later rebuilt). The large, stately brick Community Building built in Sylvan Park in 1928 at a cost of $30,000 was totally destroyed by fire on May 15, 1941. Its scaled-back replacement, at the same location, went up in 1953.

Lanesboro's most bizarre fire ignited around midnight on April 7, 2002, a major downtown blaze that ultimately destroyed three historic buildings, an outfitters shop, an ice cream parlor, and the Ford dealership. Initially it looked like the fire had been brought under control, but later in the night burning embers spread to underground timbers connecting multiple buildings. Heroic volunteer firefighters struggled to save nearby structures, and they did. It they hadn't, this fire could easily have wiped out the entire east side of Parkway Ave., if not all of downtown.

The fire had started in a back alley. But how? That question was the center of local coffee shop talk for days. All the usual suspects were named, as in "those kids." Then the truth came out, and it was a shocker, to put it mildly. John Tuchek, who

Lanesboro's Community Hall, built in 1928 for $30,000, burned down in 1941, and was replaced by the present Community Center in 1953.

just happened to be the chief of police in Lanesboro, confessed that he started the fire. He did it, he explained, to rescue—and impress—a lady friend (ex-lady friend, really) living in the upstairs apartment of the targeted building. His "hero fire" strategy, familiar to arson investigators, went awry when what he had planned to be a "small fire" ignited gas lines. Tuchek was arrested, convicted, and spent time in prison. Lives were threatened, historic buildings destroyed, businesses harmed, but thankfully no one was injured. The empty lot next to the Galligan Building (recently christened "Parkway Place") remains a sad and lasting scar of a truly bizarre event.

Railroads helped build Lanesboro. They also provided a little drama. On February 6, 1875, less than a decade after trains first pulled into town, Lanesboro had its first train wreck. Two, in fact. On that winter Saturday a train derailed just east of town. A group of workers (with a few spectators along for the ride) boarded a second train on Sunday to reach the site to begin clean-up work. On their return trip, while crossing a railroad bridge near town, apparently too quickly, the train's caboose jumped the track and plummeted off that bridge, taking a two-story fall onto frozen ground. Miraculously, eight people in the caboose escaped serious injury and returned home with quite a story.

Yes, Lanesboro is beautiful and quiet. Most of the time. But bad things can happen in good towns. This one is no exception.

A group of volunteer firefighters—the "Carrolton Guards"—protected the township in the 1870s.

The CCC Boys: "We Can Do It!"

"I'll never forget the CCC camp. It made a lot of good men."
Robert (Bob) Olson, Lanesboro CCC Boy

Two events happened in Lanesboro in 1933—one a closing, one an opening—that dramatically revealed this little town's connection to the bigger world. The first was the closing of the Lanesboro Canning Company, producer of a popular line of canned vegetables (including "Lanesboro Pride Corn") and a provider of local jobs since 1903. What happened? The Great Depression. Over the course of just a few years, the markets for Lanesboro Canning products shriveled up like the discarded corn husks on its factory floor. Once closed, the Company closed forever.

The second event, on April 27, 1933, was the opening of Lanesboro's Civilian Conservation Corps (CCC) camp. 200 young men, a few of them local, the majority from Nebraska and Missouri, assembled at the camp—officially CCC Company #751—to live and work. What they accomplished in their own lives, in the communities they served, for their families, and for their country, became one of the great success stories of 20th century America.

The CCC, the most popular of President Franklin Roosevelt's New Deal "alphabet-soup" programs, was created to help fight the Great Depression by putting young men to work on conservation projects and by supporting American families. Between 1933 and 1940, nearly three million unemployed men ages 17-28 from relief families served in the program. Each CCC boy received room-and-board, uniforms, and $30 a month, of which they were required to send $25 home to their families. Nearly 15 million American families left welfare rolls through that support. Lanesboro's CCC camp was one of 135 in Minnesota, including others in nearby Houston, Caledonia, Spring Valley and Chatfield.

The boys' nicknames, "Roosevelt's Tree Army" and "Soil Soldiers," said it all. They planted trees (more than 3 billion nationwide), completed anti-erosion projects, did bridge and dam repair, as well as road construction and maintenance. It was tough work for little pay (they called themselves "Dollar-a-Day Boys"), but they

90% of the CCC boys were from farm backgrounds.

loved it, bringing a lively and exuberant spirit to their daily work and camp life. Their self-chosen motto captured it best: "We Can Do It!" And they did.

Lanesboro's first CCC camp, a tent-city a mile south of town on Highway 16, was soon upgraded to four large wooden barracks. The CCC was a "military" operation run by reserve officers of the U.S. Army. Everyone wore uniforms (World War I surplus mostly). Schedules were regimented. An early morning bugle revile woke the camp for exercises at 6 a.m. Work started at 7:45. The days were long, the work was hard.

Evenings and weekends were for relaxation and play. The boys took part in baseball leagues, tournaments (volleyball and ping pong were popular), musical concerts and talent shows. The boys organized bands, published a camp newspaper, and started their own library. Two nights a week they'd play basketball in the Lanesboro school gym. Three other nights the boys were allowed to eat in downtown restaurants and see a movie. On Sundays they attended local churches.

CCC camp, Lanesboro

Having 200 young men living in such close proximity to a small town was bound to have an impact. Most of it was positive. Local farmers and tradesmen came to the camp to train the young men in various work-skills. The money that the boys spent in town at the movies or in restaurants helped businesses struggling to stay open. One fire-related story described CCC boys rushing into town to help put out a fire at the White Front Café on Parkway. (A rumor that the fire had started by CCC boys trying to siphon gas so they could get back to meet curfew didn't diminish their efforts).

"We worked hard but we had fun, too," remembers one Lanesboro CCC boy. "We enjoyed mingling with local kids, the girls especially. CCC leaders knew what they were doing, though. They'd move guys around various camps and kept a good eye on us!" Lanesboro CCC reunions, held for years afterward, overflowed with fun stories and a few fairy-tale endings. A number of CCC boys did meet local girls, fell in love, eventually got married, even raised families here. One of the young men, Eldor Rahn, married a Lanesboro girl, and decades later their son, Steve, became town mayor.

By 1942, the world was changing. The U.S., fully engaged in World War II after Pearl Harbor, was invading Europe. Young men who years earlier would have been candidates for the CCC were now enlisting. The nation's economy was recovering and the need for relief efforts like the CCC was diminishing. In the early 1940's, the last CCC boys in the Lanesboro camp dismantled the barracks that had been their home.

Signs of hard work by CCC boys in and around Lanesboro are still visible today. The boys built the Inspiration Point Roadside Rest on Highway 16 on the way to Preston. They placed still-standing stone-and-cement walls along nearby highways and behind the Sons of Norway Lodge on Parkway Avenue. They erected bridges across local streams, built a retaining wall along Gribbon Creek and made valuable contributions to soil-saving projects all across Fillmore County. They spent one entire summer constructing a small dam on a steam north of Preston that still stands today.

Two fun CCC shadows remain. Look close at the brick wall on Parkway (now the site of the Iron Horse motorcycle store) and you'll find graffiti-signatures (and dates) left by CCC boys. Drive south on Highway 16 to their former camp site (once again a dairy farm) and you'll see the two sets of granite steps, one on each side of the road that once led to CCC Camp #751.

Take a moment while you're there. Close your eyes. Use your imagination. Listen for the sounds of a lively camp filled with hundreds of young men talking, laughing, playing baseball, maybe a small group singing, or hungry young men heading to a

Some Lanesboro CCC boys earned diplomas through Lanesboro High School.

mess hall. Maybe the sound of a day-closing trumpet. We should remember—even honor—the "We Can Do It!" spirit in this group of ordinary young men who worked in extraordinary ways in a dark and difficult time. Big world stuff, in a little town called Lanesboro.

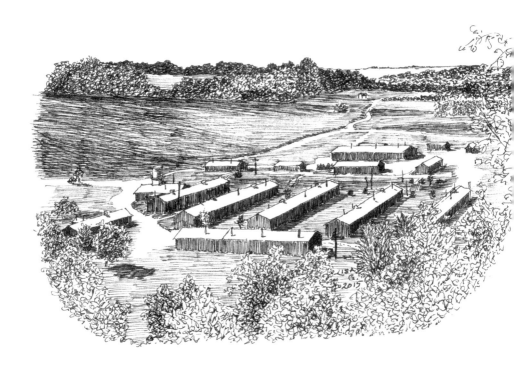

Lanesboro CCC Camp Barracks

Another nickname for the CCC boys was the "Colossal College of Calluses."

M.O. Bue

"Bue was more than a picture taker. He was an artist."
Randolph Huss

How do you best discover Lanesboro history? You can browse thousands of items at the Lanesboro History Museum. (An admiring tourist once described it to me as "a delightful little museum that has a hard time saying no.") You can get a walking tour map and hit the streets. Books help. So does visiting with locals at a local coffee shop. Lanesboro has a colorful history and it's very accessible.

M.O. Bue self portrait

Maybe the best way to explore Lanesboro history is to spend some time appreciating the work of Matias O. Bue, Lanesboro's most famous—and beloved—photographer.

Bue was born in Norway in 1889. At the age of 18 in 1907 he followed his older brother to Minnesota and found work as a farmhand first in Yellow Medicine County and later in Granite Falls. Photography grabbed him early. On one of those Minnesota farms where he worked, he transformed a rustic shed into his first "photo studio." For Matias Bue, his hobby became his passion and eventually his life-long career.

His timing was excellent. He was born one year after George

"You have not seen Minnesota if you have not seen the Root River Valley." (M.O. Bue)

Kodak invented his famous camera. As he grew up and developed an interest in photography, new technology was making picture-taking easier. New markets for photos were also emerging. Thousands of settlers and immigrants in the American west were eager to buy photos of themselves to mail back home. ("Photo postcards," the first "selfies," came along and helped meet that demand.) Enterprising young photographers like Bue began taking—and selling—pictures in small towns across America.

You can see why Bue was attracted to Lanesboro. The town had a history of successful photographers. Hanson opened a studio in the 1870s (his work included portraits of Buffalo Bill) and was followed by T.F. Bergasel in 1887. Lanesboro's vibrant Norwegian culture no doubt also felt very welcoming to Bue, a young man just five years removed from "the old country." In 1912 he decided to make his home here.

Quickly planting roots, Bue bought the Bergasel Photo Studio, joined the Kiwanis and Odd Fellows clubs, served on the City Council, and was a charter member of the Sons of Norway Lodge. In 1915 he married a local girl, Susanna Larson. Bue's photo business flourished, leading him to soon buy a bigger building, add a gift shop, and expand his basement dark room. The Bue photo studio soon became, according to the Lanesboro Leader, "the busiest place in town."

He excelled in studio portraits but also enjoyed working at weddings, church events, and town gatherings. One colleague said Bue "...carried a camera with him everywhere he went and took pictures of everything that struck his fancy." He took pictures at every school within a 50-mile radius of Lanesboro. His Model A Coupe, with a custom-designed trunk strapped to its side carrying his camera and tripod was a familiar sight on dirt roads throughout Fillmore County.

Bue took his craft seriously. He hiked for miles through bluff country to find just the right vantage point for landscape shots. His exquisite scenes of Sylvan Park in winter and of the Lanesboro Dam look like paintings and are as stunning today as when he first developed them in his Parkway Ave. dark room a century ago. A night-time, Ansel Adams-like photograph he took of Church Hill from across Mill Pond has a ghostly glow at its center. Bue gave it a title—"Moon Rise"—and signed it, not common practices for photographers of that day, hinting at the artistic pride he took in his work.

Bue also loved capturing "everyday" Lanesboro: folks walking down Main Street, working on their farms, relaxing in their homes, even playing croquet on their front lawns. A Bue photo brings Lanesboro's past to life. A cleverly-angled picture of Pete Kvernum at work in his 1920 barber shop captures both barber and customer. Another shows Claude Williams playfully pulling his brother, Clarence, in a cart down Parkway Ave., both smiling broadly.

You can see parallels between Bue's work and that of his contemporary, the famed illustrator Norman Rockwell. Both men had a gift for story-telling, through photos (Bue) and paintings (Rockwell) filled with warmth and humor. Place Rockwell's comical self-portrait painting next to Bue's self-portrait photo (with a camera curtain draped over his head) and you can't help but think these guys would have liked each other. They also shared a genius for capturing American images that decades later remain as timely and lively as tomorrow's tweet.

Bue sold his Lanesboro photo business in 1946, ran his gift shop for another eight years, then lived a quiet retirement until his passing in 1969 at the age of 80. The town mourned the loss of this solid citizen, friendly neighbor, good friend—and world-class photographer. In the early 1930s, the Bue Studio and Gift Shop entered a float in the town's July 4th parade display this theme: "Photographs Live Forever." Thankfully, because of the photographs—yes, the art—of Matias O. Bue, the same can be said for more than three decades of Lanesboro history.

"Langlie Bros. store being moved." (1923)

Better Days Behind...and Ahead

"Main Street isn't main street anymore.
Lights don't shine as brightly as they shone before."
Randy Newman, "Our Town"

The Lanesboro story would be better, I suppose, if all we said about this little town was that it was founded by inspired people and that it flourished from day one to the present. That would make a more positive story. But it wouldn't be true.

The truth is that Lanesboro—like thousands of other small, rural American towns—has faced struggles, difficult times, and uncertainties. It began as a boomtown but by the early 1900s a series of crop failures and national economic upheavals had weakened early enthusiasm. The 1918 flu epidemic and World War I were harsh realities everywhere, including Lanesboro. Life went on, families made the best of things. But after the Great Depression, World War II, the ending of rail traffic in the 1960s, and the farm crisis of the 1970s, this community was on the ropes.

Parkway Avenue storefronts were increasingly empty in those years. "Back then you could have bought this whole town for $100,000," a local once told me. Maybe that's a stretch, but even if close to true, it makes a statement. I also heard the reason most of the original buildings still stand on Parkway Avenue is that no one had the money to fix them up or to tear them down. Most properties were in passive disrepair. Population continued to decline. There was talk of school consolidations. "Will this town survive?" became a tough question that no one wanted to face.

By the late 1970s Lanesboro had lost its early energy. Some even called it a "ghost town." But many good people still lived, worked, farmed, and raised families here. A rich vein of community pride persevered. The Lanesboro School successfully fought to remain independent. Yes, there were tough times. Tough decades even. But Lanesboro hung in there. And better days were definitely ahead.

"Subscribers are requested to please see that children are not allowed to play with the phones as this greatly annoys the operators." (F & M Telephone instructions printed in the Lanesboro Leader in 1916)

Rails-to-Trails Rekindles A Town

The unexpected story has a happy ending.

By the middle of the 20th century, American railroads were in decline. Deregulation rocked the industry. Lines were being shortened, shut down, even abandoned. That was true for southern Minnesota, Fillmore County, and for Lanesboro. As mentioned earlier, trains stopped running here in the early 1970s.

What would happen to now abandoned railroad tracks and the property they sat on? In some parts of the country, people began to use them as walking paths. No big national movement, just people informally doing something they enjoyed on newly accessible land.

Discussions started around this issue across the country. Could newly-abandoned railroad lines be transformed into public, multi-use trails? A first attempt was made in 1965 when Wisconsin purchased the right-of-way to the Chicago-North Western Railway and opened the 32-mile Elroy-Sparta Trail. Featuring three historic railroad tunnels, it's now considered the first successful rail-to-trail initiative in the United States.

Next door in Minnesota similar talk began. In July, 1979, the "Milwaukee Road Corridor Area Feasibility Study" was completed. Before long a handful of legislative leaders proposed turning a portion of the abandoned Milwaukee Road rail line in southeastern Minnesota into a multi-use trail that would pass through the towns of Fountain, Whalan, Peterson, Rushford—and Lanesboro. By 1981 the state purchased 49 miles of that rail bed for $975,000. Momentum was building—at least in St. Paul.

How did the people of Lanesboro react to the idea of a trail here? Was it immediately and universally endorsed? Did it become another example of the town's inspiring, visionary, can-do spirit? That's the story I expected to hear and write when I began this book. It would make a good story. Except that it's not true.

Local support for a trail through Lanesboro in the early to mid-1970s was weak at best. There was active opposition, in fact. Who was against the idea? Many local farmers and landowners. (One early survey showed 75% rejected it). It's not hard

By the 1970s rail traffic had slowed with trains sometimes arriving here only a few times each month.

to understand why. The old railroad lines passed through their property. If that land was now available, they wanted it.

Those same people—others, too—also worried about the impact a bike trail might have. How would a multi-use trail affect the farms it passed through? A trail would bring unknown people—who? how many? when? why?—onto their land. Was there a danger of increased trespassing, litter, even vandalism, from bike-riding tourists? What field access problems would a trail create? How would long-festering fencing issues be solved? Many of those unanswered questions led to local (and loud) meetings. Groups were formed, lawyers were called. It became difficult and contentious.

Fast forward a few years. Hard discussions eventually led to deals and compromises. (Minnesota State Senator Jerry Gunderson from Mabel played a key role in those discussions). Funding was approved and a plan was adopted. Lanesboro, bluff country at large, would have a trail. Construction began by the mid-'80s, and in 1988 the first riders hit its pavement, riding from Rushford to Lanesboro. In 1997, $6-million additional bonding funds led to the completion of the Harmony-Preston Trail. By 2000, bikers were enjoying a 60-mile trail that connects Fountain, Lanesboro, Whalan, Peterson, Rushford and Houston, as well as Preston and Harmony.

Today the Rails-to-Trails Conservancy estimates that there are 22,000 miles of trails like this across the U.S. The Root River State Trail, used primarily for biking, but also for hiking and cross-country skiing, has become one of the most popular and most scenic biking destinations in the state. Early opponents came to welcome it. Fears about litter and vandalism never materialized. The Root River State Trail is now credited with helping revitalize the town of Lanesboro. Now that is a fun and true story to tell!

Early Lanesboro bikers

Crown Prince (later King Olaf) of Norway and his wife, Martha, visited Lanesboro in 1939.

Tom McGuigan

An out-of-towner mends all kinds of fences.

This man wasn't born here and lived only briefly in Rochester. Originally from Massachusetts, he now makes his home in Guilford, Connecticut. In the past thirty years he's returned to Lanesboro just a handful of times to fish and bike the trail. If you passed him on a local street, you wouldn't recognize him. But we really should get to know him.

Tom McGuigan had just finished college when he was hired in January, 1981, by the Minnesota Department of Natural Resources to be the first manager of the Root River Trail. Over the course of three pivotal years, Tom served as the DNR's "boots on the ground" in the pre-construction phase of the Root River State Trail. He played a low-key role, he admits, and stayed mostly in the background. But the work that Tom McGuigan did played a key role in the trail's beginning, in its early success, and in Lanesboro's powerful resurgence in the 1990s.

As we said earlier, the idea of turning abandoned rail lines into public, multi-use trails was fairly new in the 1970s. We also learned that the idea of doing that here with the Southern Minnesota Railroad line was not immediately well-received. Years of discussion, contentious debate, political wrangling, and hard-worked compromises led to final approval by the Minnesota Legislature. Like it or not, and many still didn't like it back then, there would be a Root River State Trail.

Into that agitated mix stepped young Tom McGuigan with these directions from his DNR bosses: get on-site and get the trail started. That was no slam dunk, however.

"When I arrived I was under the impression that there was some local support for the trail," Tom remembers. "Frankly, I didn't find any. Many people were still suspicious of the state and how this would go. I was sympathetic to their concerns. I also knew what the legislature had mandated and what my bosses were telling me. It was all pretty challenging, that's for sure."

Tom, a hands-on guy with a love for the outdoors, did what came natural to him. He laced up his hiking boots and walked the old rail line from Fountain to the Money Creek Woods between Rushford and Houston, about 33 miles of trail.

The Root River State Trail opened for public use in 1989.

Twice. He wanted to see for himself what was being proposed and what needed to be done. He also wanted to meet people face-to-face, especially the farmers and landowners who would be most directly affected by the proposed trail. He was warned those meetings might be tense. And they were.

"Many landowners were very upset," Tom recalls. "I remember two times when I was actually concerned for my safety. In another case a farmer had cut down trees across the trail to block our path."

Tom kept walking, kept talking, kept listening.

"We documented the most difficult issues, which were fencing and access," he says. "Farmers were suspicious of government promises, some rightly so. Some land was sold back. We did some re-routing. Mostly we kept trying to address people's concerns. I learned to repair fences and brought in a crew of Minnesota conservation corps workers and trained them to fix fences, too. On a recent visit, I saw that many of those fences we worked on are still standing."

Field access was another hot-button topic for farmers.

"Field access was a priority that had to be protected," Tom remembers. "We worked hard on that. Just west of Isinours we put in a big culvert so cattle could move between fields. That culvert is still here today, too."

Tom doggedly kept at it. Compromises were fashioned, tempers cooled, the trail moved forward. Tom McGuigan played a key role in that. A DNR summary report described him as "...a source of local knowledge and common sense." He made invaluable contributions to an inflamed situation at a crucial crossroad.

The results bear that out. Over three decades, the Root River State Trail has helped revitalize not just Lanesboro, but all the trail towns it now touches. "That's great to hear," Tom says. "I'm glad it all worked out and that so many people, both locally and from far away, have such a beautiful trail to use and enjoy."

More than 100,000 people use the Root River State Trail every year, according to the DNR.

Saying "Yes!" To the Arts

"It's safe to do art in Lanesboro."
Robbie Brokken

Lanesboro has worn many hats over the years. River town. Farm town. Boom-town. Immigrant Gateway. New ones, too, in recent years. "The Heart of Bluff Country." "The Bed & Breakfast Capital of Minnesota." All fit, for different reasons and seasons.

Here's one that sounds surprising at first. In 2013 Lanesboro was named "One of the Top 12 Small Town ArtPlaces in America," showing up on the same list as renowned places like Stowe, Vermont, Vineyard Haven, Massachusetts, and Taos, New Mexico. Lanesboro, Minnesota? Quite an honor. Does it really fit?

A leading arts organization, Americans for the Arts, says that "...a small arts town epitomizes rural cultural coolness... (where people) might stay at a gorgeous B&B, have dinner in a great (but undiscovered) restaurant, wander around art galleries, antique shops, and flea markets, or perhaps visit an annual Art in the Park festival... the sort of place where urbanites move to after selling their condo and finding a renovated farmhouse on five forested acres. On weekends these new residents enjoy art gallery openings and local musicians performing at cafes. On weeknights there are jazz concerts and dance programs at the local arts center, or maybe a Tennessee Williams play at the restored, art deco theater downtown. A small art town is the sort of place where people can find a true sense of community."

Yes, that sure sounds like Lanesboro. The hat fits.

From the 1980s on this community became a place where the arts—painting, music, theater, writing, photography, dance, sculpture, craft-making, and more— are valued, celebrated and plentiful. A place where artists live and do their creative thing. The arts are alive and growing in Lanesboro.

That's not totally new, though. Look closely and you'll find colorful threads of artistic energy woven throughout this town's history. When immigrants arrived here in the mid-19th century from places like Ireland, Germany and Norway, they brought luggage and new languages; they brought their arts and culture, too. They

"In many ways this small town 'shouldn't' work, but it does. Its great quality of life inspires the arts and just makes it a fun place to live." (Jeremy van Meter)

shared their painting, music, literature, photography, jewelry, and dance, and those gifts enhanced the entire community.

Early Lanesboro welcomed and celebrated all kinds of art. There were Sunday afternoon concerts in Sylvan Park, a "floating band" that played on the Mill Pond, church melodramas, school plays, and Norwegian-language theater at the Sons of Norway Lodge. Musical variety and vaudeville-type productions—including popular "woman-less weddings"—drew enthusiastic crowds. Young people created theatrical groups, silent movies played at the Elite Theater. Individual artists thrived, too, like Hans Olson, a barber by day, a master woodcarver in his spare time.

Why do art and Lanesboro blend so well? Many say the natural landscape around here inspires it. "This town is landlocked in scenic beauty," says John Davis, Executive Director of Lanesboro Arts. "Just looking at the bluffs, the river, the forests, the rolling hills helps artists flourish here."

The welcome that artists find here also helps. Robbie Brokken, an artist herself, has been involved in the local art scene for 13 years and now serves as director of the Lanesboro Arts gallery. "Creative people are compelled to create," Robbie says. "In Lanesboro they find a supportive community that supports their healthy compulsion. Many artists gravitate here. It's also an affordable place to live and artists like that."

Local artistic spirit blossomed in the early 1980s with the formation of the Lanesboro Arts Council. It was the Council that encouraged local student-actor Eric Bunge to try a summer play season and rented the St. Mane Theater to him (for $1). That push gave birth to the Commonweal Theatre, a local and regional artistic gem that will soon begin its 30th season. The Council also started an annual Art in the Park festival and promoted gallery exhibitions. In 1993 the Cornucopia Arts Center was organized to provide networking-support and gallery space for local artists.

"Back then locals didn't know quite what to do with all this art-talk," remembers Julia Borgen, a long-time Lanesboro resident. "You'd hear people making fun of it. But that's all changed. In the last 30 years arts have become a welcome and vital part of the entire town."

In 2010 the Lanesboro Arts Council and Cornucopia merged to become Lanesboro Arts Center which today (as Lanesboro Arts) offers a gallery showcasing the juried work of nearly 100 artists from Minnesota, Wisconsin, and Iowa. The gallery also presents artist exhibitions 5-6 times a year, more than 30 concert and film events at the St. Mane Theater annually, a live-radio community variety show called "Over the Back Fence" (now in its 23rd year), artist-in-residence opportunities, special shows (like Catherine Glynn's recent production of "Audacious Raw Theater"), public art projects like community murals, "Surprise Sculpture" each summer with Lanesboro kids, and more. Earlier this year a partnership with the Smithsonian brought the traveling "Water/Ways" exhibit here, one of only six places where it was shown in the state.

Add to that the Commonweal Theater season, winter and summer productions by the Lanesboro Community Theater, History Alive! Lanesboro pop-up plays each fall, a variety of concerts in the Sons of Norway Hall, sold-out Holiday Sing-a-Longs with Twin Cities musician Dan Chouinard, bi-annual Art Crawls, the annual String-wood Chamber Music Festival (featuring youth concerts), the spring-time Bluff Country Gathering for folk and old-time music, and you can see why Lanesboro more than earns its art reputation.

In September, 2014, Lanesboro's City Council passed a unanimous resolution declaring the entire town an Arts Campus, the first rural town in America to do so. "What that means," says Davis, "is that the entire town, not just one facility, is a canvas for the arts. It creates a new way of looking at our community, of seeing every square inch of this place as an arts center. Our vision is to engage all people here in the arts in some way."

Barbara Benson (Bebe) Keith, a multi-talented artist, actor and author, moved to Lanesboro ten years ago with her husband, Pete. Bebe's mosaics and sculptures are displayed in children's hospitals across the United States (including Children's in Boston and Gillette in St. Paul), as well as at the Minneapolis/St. Paul International Airport, the University of Iowa, Augsburg College and the Mayo Clinic. In Lanesboro she creates art, acts in and directs LCT plays, writes books, produces films, and hosts a local arts-related cable TV show. Why she does all that embodies the artistic energy here.

"I can't imagine a life without creativity," Bebe says. "It's what I do every day. It's what keeps me going and excited for the future. When I set out on a creative endeavor, I'm invigorated. When it's completed, I'm proud. Then I start thinking about what comes next. It gives me energy and so many 'feel good' moments. To me, that's what life is all about!"

In 2014 Lanesboro Arts received a major Bush Prize for Community Innovation for its role in developing the Lanesboro Arts Campus initiative.

The arts work in Lanesboro. They have even helped revive the economy of this once fading rural town, catching the attention of similar communities that are looking to learn from that model.

You catch the "feel" of this town's art energy at an event like "Silent Movies in the Park." It's a Sunday evening in mid-September. I'm sitting in a lawn chair in quiet and peaceful Sylvan Park with about 50 other people, wearing sweatshirts and bundled in blankets against the fall chill. We're waiting for it to get dark so we can watch films on the big screen set up in front. It's even fun waiting. Tom Schramm is strumming his guitar and leading a group sing-a-long. Popcorn (50 cents a bag) is popping, friendly dogs stop for a pat, neighbors visit. Sylvan Park suddenly feels like a cozy living room filled with family and friends ready to enjoy some home movies.

We'll see six silent films tonight, each about six minutes long each, totally produced by local folks who develop the ideas, create the captions, do the filming and editing, and add music. It's all free, donations accepted. (A state arts grant helps, too.) The movies are mostly re-fashioned fairy tales and the audience happily responds when familiar faces and scenery appear on screen. We applaud the filmmakers afterward and you sense their pride in trying something creative, something brand new.

People seek art in Lanesboro. They visit galleries, enjoy paintings, attend plays, and listen to concerts. They support local artists. Regular people here can also be artists. They make silent movies. Act in community theater. Take water-color classes. Do skits, tell jokes and sing at "Over the Back Fence." Play guitar at the High Court Pub's "open mic" nights. Square dance at Sons of Norway Barn Dances. Learn felting at an Eagle Bluff Skills School class. Break little pieces of glass for mosaics on a downtown wall. So much to explore, learn about, and enjoy. And to try. In Lanesboro, art is a participatory sport. It's a hat this town wears proudly.

In 2016 Lanesboro high school students Mai Gjere, Olivia Obritsch, and Nora Sampson, created short films about Lanesboro as part of the Smithsonian Institute's "Stories from Main Street" project.

A Prairie Home on a Softball Field

"Lanesboro is enough like Lake Wobegon to remind me of where I came from."
Garrison Keillor

"Prairie Home Companion," the radio variety show created by and featuring Garrison Keillor, was a Saturday night fixture on national public radio for 40 years on more than 700 stations. The show normally broadcast live from St. Paul's Fitzgerald Theater. Over the years it also originated from big-time venues like New York City's Town Hall, the Ryman Auditorium in Nashville, and the Greek Theater in Los Angeles. Nearly four million people tuned in weekly.

But "Prairie Home" may never have felt more at home than it did one rainy Saturday evening in June, 2007, when it originated from Lanesboro's softball field. It was a night this little town, and no doubt Keillor himself, will never forget.

How did the show find its way here? Keillor had visited Lanesboro a few times previously, had even done a bit of political fundraising here. As a lover of rural America and all-things rhubarb (he's the composer of "Be Bop-A-Rebop, Rhubarb Pie," after all) his attraction to the place seemed a natural fit. Nancy Martinson, Head Stalk of the Divine Rhubarb Committee, extended him an invitation to visit the Rhubarb Festival which planted a (rhubarb?) seed. Ideas were floated, schedulers consulted, and it was agreed that not only would Keillor visit the Festival, he'd do his live radio show from here. That presented a huge technical undertaking. The "in house" audience alone would nearly triple the town's entire population. But in classic Lanesboro fashion an enthusiastic can-do spirit kicked in and a date was set for June 2, 2007.

The biggest challenge turned out to be the weather. June is stormy in Minnesota. Turbulent thunderstorms, even tornadoes, are not uncommon. When Keillor, the show's cast, special musical guests, and a team of support people arrived here late in the week to erect a stage, plug in plugs, and rehearse, forecasts looked ominous. Friday's rehearsal would be taped and that would come in handy, but that's getting ahead of ourselves.

"Won't you come over and see me sometime? Eat your breakfast before you start. Bring your dinner in your hand. And leave before suppertime." (lyrics from a Bob Bovee song at the June, 2007 "Prairie Home Companion" show in Lanesboro)

The Rhubarb Festival, then in its third year, provided a perfect backdrop for the show, starting Saturday morning when Keillor happily mingled with festival-goers in Sylvan Park, posed for pictures, and eagerly sampled local rhubarb delicacies. By late afternoon long lines of people carrying lawn chairs, blankets, and umbrellas began snaking towards the softball field. That was about the same time that large thunderheads, swollen black with rain, came rolling over the bluffs of the Root River Valley.

Winds picked up, raindrops started falling, and those umbrellas popped open. Announcements were made about storm watches and warnings to the now-fidgety crowd. People were given friendly nudges to head for cover if they felt inclined. A few did. Most stayed put, wetter by the minute but smiling. Keillor, microphone in hand, walked into the crowd, and pretty much got soaked himself. He was nothing but cheerful, though, sang improvised lyrics to "You Are My Sunshine" ("...even if it rains, let's all stay put"), high-fived a few locals, even danced with some kids.

Keillor dried off, changed clothes and went on stage. The show, he said, would go on if at all possible. It was and it did. The show's lineup included Texas singer-songwriter Joe Ely and the Guy's All-Star Show Band featuring pianist Rich Dworsky. Local connections were obvious crowd favorites. Bob Bovee and Gail Heil sang. Orv and Marie Amdahl, whose white farmhouse sits high above the town on Lanesboro's north bluff, were invited on stage to celebrate their 65th anniversary, and danced to a waltz that Dworsky composed just for them. The Rhubarb Sisters (then Peggy Hanson, Julie Kiehne, and Stella Burdt) harmonized perfectly with the host on a rousing rendition of his rhubarb song. Lanesboro High School student Yvonne Freese, 16, wowed the audience with her solo soprano talent.

The downpours held off, musical interludes ended, and Keillor shared his weekly Lake Wobegone monologue. (His clever reference to a "fictional" police officer starting a fire to win back a lost love elicited knowing home-town chuckles.) A little more music, a heart-felt farewell ("we're not going to get over Lanesboro for a very long time," he said), and this rainy but magical night came to a happy end.

Few people knew, some never found out, that the threat of heavy rain, lightning, thunder, and possible power outages, made it too risky to broadcast the show live. So while the local crowd enjoyed Saturday's in-person show, the national radio audience was listening to Friday night's taped rehearsal. Same guests, songs, skits, sound effects and Wobegone stories. It all worked fine.

Having a special guest in town, not to mention the national exposure of the Prairie Home show, was a thrill and a memory-maker for Lanesboro. The way everyone handled threatening skies with smiles and steadiness only added flavor to the entire event. It made Lanesboro, Minnesota—where the women here are strong, too, the men (most of them, anyway) are good looking, and the children, well, if they aren't all above average, are still great kids who sure do try their best—seem even more like a place you'd be proud to call home.

C.O. Hubell, Lanesboro Blacksmith, 1900

Arnold Rank caught rattlesnakes here for a county-paid bounty, once nabbing 48 in a single day, 286 in one year, and more than 2,000 snakes over 40 years! He caught one diamond back rattler that was seven feet long and had 16 rattles.

Gutzom Would, Too

Who belongs on Mt. Lanesboro?

I said Gertrude Stein would love Lanesboro because of its "there," its distinct sense of place. I think Gutzom Borglum would love it here, too. He's the famous sculptor who carved the four presidential faces on Mt. Rushmore. I don't know if limestone would work as well as South Dakota rock cliffs, but Lanesboro's bluffs seem like a good location for a "Mt. Lanesboro!"

So...who should be on it? If Borglum was still around to do a project like that (he's not, he died in 1941), what four faces should be chosen for Mt. Lanesboro to honor them for the impact they had on this town?

We've met a number of good candidates already. Michael Scanlan and O.M. Habberstad both have inspiring, rags-to-riches immigrant stories that certainly qualify them as town "founders." Thomas Brayton played a key role in actually building early Lanesboro. Men like Buffalo Bill and M.O. Bue, in different eras for different reasons, left their mark here. Much later, the huge impact of the Root River Trail could even justify putting young Tom McGuigan on that rock-face.

Before I share my personal choices—and welcome you to agree or disagree—here are more nominations for Mt. Lanesboro.

Robert R. Greer, Lanesboro's first mayor, was born on a farm in Quebec, Canada in 1842, but made it here—by way of Decorah and La Crosse—by the time he was 26. Greer and his cousin J.C. built one of the first downtown buildings and opened the Greer Dry Good Store, a fixture in Lanesboro for nearly 40 years. R.R. and his wife, Sadie, helped the town grow in another way—they had 10 kids! Greer later became a state legislator (as did his two sons, Harry and Herbert) and moved to St. Paul in 1905.

Samuel A. Nelson was born in Norway in 1851 and immigrated here as a teenager. He and Olie Langlie started a general store. Later with his brother, Peter, Samuel started the Farmers & Merchants Bank of Lanesboro that became the First National Bank of Lanesboro. A tireless volunteer, Nelson became President of the Norwegian Pioneer Association and, like Greer, served in both houses of the Min-

Dennis Galligan, a railroad contractor who helped build the Canadian Pacific Railway and railroads for James J. Hill, moved here in 1867.

nesota Legislature. Also like Greer, he and his wife, Julie, raised ten children in their impressive Victorian home at 709 Parkway Ave. S. Nelson passed away in 1939.

Lanesboro has had its share of able and memrable physicians (not even counting Dr. "White Beaver" Powell). A contemporary of Powell's, **Dr. Johan Hvoslef** had a distinguished 50-year career here, and like Powell, Dr. Hvoslef's fame traveled beyond the medical exam room. A self-trained ornithologist, Hvoslef became known as "The Bird Doctor of Lanesboro," taking long walks in Root River Valley forests and fields to gather extensive notes on local birds that were eventually donated to the University of Minnesota's Bell Museum of Natural History where they are still in use today.

Dr. Ralph Bernard (R.B.) Johnson arrived in Lanesboro in 1931. In 1945, with his wife, Edna, a nurse, by his side, Doc Johnson established his own "hospital" in the Victorian home built by Issac Vickerman on the corner of Pleasant and Calhoun. (You'll still meet people today who proudly tell you they were born in that house). Doc Johnson, who founded the March of Dimes in Fillmore County, closed his hospital in 1966 and started a clinic downtown before his retirement.

Rose (Horihan) Bell was raised on a family farm north of town, graduated from Lanesboro High School in 1932, left for college, but returned with her husband, Ted, to teach English at her alma mater for nearly 25 years. She was school librarian, served the Lanesboro Public Library board for 51 years, and was an active member/volunteer at St. Patrick's Church.

Rose Bell loved her hometown, her students, her church—and books. "I grew up on the street where she lived," remembers one former student. "Mrs. Bell's lights were always on late at night because she loved to read. She passed her enthusiasm to us. Her class was like a book club and we loved it." Another former student, Minnesota lawyer and later judge, Carol Person, agrees. "Mrs. Bell saw only promise in her students and expected the best of us."

Lanesboro celebrated Rose Bell's career as dedicated school teacher and community volunteer by making her Grand Marshall of the Buffalo Bill Days parade one year and with the "Rose Bell Reading Room" in the town library. She passed away at age 93 in 2009.

Don Ward grew up in Lanesboro. Later, his work as an engineer took him from here, but upon his return Don's love for his hometown and its history–spurred by "treasures" he found in local garage and estate sales–had not dimmed. He bought the original Bue Studio downtown with thoughts of becoming a serious photographer.

"Don soon realized that spending all that time in a dark room wasn't for him," says Gene Bergstrom, a long-time Lanesboro friend. "He moved on from that."

Ward stayed active in promoting Lanesboro and its history. He was one of the organizers of Buffalo Bill Days and other town events. He was a driving force in establishing the Lanesboro History Museum, eventually donating more than 700 items to the Museum. His organization of early Lanesboro records, newspapers and photos is a remarkable and lasting achievement.

"Without Don Ward, there wouldn't be a Lanesboro history," says Bergstrom, "or at the least we wouldn't know much about it. He did a tremendous amount of work. Everyone who cares about this town and its history benefits from that."

As of this writing, Don Ward (who spent part of his childhood in the house where I now live) resides in Onalaska, Wisconsin. He is in his 90's and in declining health. But the vibrancy of Don's love for his hometown lives on in the contributions he made to preserve its history. Lanesboro's history—the priceless stories of its past and its people—remain for the generations yet to enjoy this place. That's true, thanks to Don Ward.

I'm sure other great candidates could be nominated for Mt. Lanesboro. Here are my four choices. See what you think.

A solid representative of so many courageous, talented and hard-working immigrants who helped start this town...**Michael Scanlan.**

A colorful trailblazer for so many who have brought a dash of creative entrepreneurship to this town, a spirit that definitely lives on today...**Dr. Frank (White Beaver) Powell.**

A champion of artistic excellence (another on-going town quality) and a role model of a good citizen...**M.O. Bue.**

A man whose love for his hometown and its history left Lanesboro a priceless gift...**Don Ward.**

Okay, let's find some chisels and get to work!

"Please do not spit on the floor. Remember the Johnstown Flood." (A slide in an early Lanesboro silent movie house).

Lanesboro... Its Places

Lanesboro Town Hall...1886

Fillmore County—established on March 5, 1853—was named after U.S. President Millard Fillmore (1850-1853).

Lanesboro...Its Places

On the north wall of the Pedal Pushers Café building on the corner of Parkway Avenue and Coffee Street you'll find a set of river-themed mosaics created in 2017 by St. Paul artist Bailey Cahlander. They're beautiful and create a perfect backdrop to the nearby sounds of the rushing Root River.

A mosaic fits Lanesboro. This whole town is a mosaic, a collection of many different places. Some highlight the natural beauty and God-created physical wonders of this place. A flowing river, towering bluffs, and rolling hills draw people here to be refreshed and inspired.

Lanesboro's man-made places are also compelling. Historic architecture abounds downtown. Old neighborhoods are filled with elegant homes fun to look at and learn about. If you like taking photos, you'll find more than enough subjects to fill your lens. That's especially true when you slow down to capture the details.

Lanesboro also has places that are "experiences," the often unplanned, spontaneous connections that happen around here all the time. Bits of conversation between local and tourist on a sidewalk or in a café. A brief but moving encounter with a piece of art in a gallery or shop. An unexpected touch of emotion or insight you take from the stage of a theater. They can turn out to be the most personal and lasting of all of its simple pleasures.

Open your eyes, your ears, and your imagination, to the places of Lanesboro. You'll be amazed at what you discover.

Lanesboro's first school was built in 1870 on Church Hill.

A Walk Through Lanesboro

"I think of Lanesboro as having all the things that make a neighborhood special.
And you can pretty much walk to everything."
Jennifer Wood

Lanesboro was originally platted with five sections: Downtown, Church Hill, Brooklyn, Little Norway, and the Flat. It made an easy way to direct folks before streets and numbers. ("You know, the Johnsons. They live down in the Flat.") Those neighborhoods all still exist. The town is small enough, its slopes gentle enough (Church Hill the one exception), that given a nice day and comfortable shoes, it's very walkable. Let's do it!

Downtown   The brick buildings in Downtown Lanesboro don't just look old—they are old. Most were constructed in the late 1800s. A number are on the National Register of Historic Places. The entire downtown—bisected by a street first called "E," then "Main," now "Parkway"—is like a building museum, home to the town's earliest hotels, saloons, stores, banks, and restaurants. Here are a few highlights:

The Pedal Pushers Café building (121 Parkway Ave. N., 1867), first a saloon, it later housed the Nelson brothers' Farmers & Merchants Bank, the Lanesboro Benevolent Society, and a grocery store. Glass-lettering in its front windows dates to its time as Hanson's Drugs (1933-1973). The opposite corner to the south of the same block is **Mrs. B's Historic Lanesboro Inn** (101 Parkway Ave. N., 1872), the long-time home of Thompson Brothers Furniture. (The brothers, who ran a mortuary as well, made caskets in this building. Maybe that's explains why ghost stories aren't uncommon here). **The High Court Pub** (109 Parkway Ave. N., 1870s), Parkway's only three-story building, was the town's courthouse (1876-1916) presided over by the Honorable J.G. French, Lanesboro's mutton-chopped Justice of the Peace.

Directly across from Pedal Pushers on the corner of Coffee Street and Parkway (118 Parkway Ave. N., 1923) is a building that's served as a bank under various names and owners for nearly a century. Lanesboro's can-do spirit also helped make that true. In 1923 the Scanlan-Habberstad Bank wanted this prominent spot, but the Langlie Brothers Grocery & Confectionary already occupied it. Scanlan-Habberstad

The Devy Hotel (1870-1940s), now often called "The Blue Hotel," later run by the Thoens, was the last of Lanesboro's original hotels still in operation.

bought the lot anyway, moved Langlies sixty-five feet to the south, and built their new bank. Langlies later became the studio/gift shop of photographer Matias O. Bue. Currently it is the Root River Rod Company. (Look for Bue's original shop sign hanging inside).

The **Galligan Building** (108 Parkway Ave. N., 1895) was home to a bank, a newspaper, and the Post Office from 1950-1962. Also called "the Opera House," it had a large hall upstairs used for various community gatherings. The **Old Village Hall Restaurant and Pub** (111 Coffee Street, 1886) once held town offices, the police department, the firehouse (until 1966), and jail. (Its bars remain in the back window). Now a popular restaurant, this building was also the site of the town's first historical museum.

Other historic Downtown buildings include the Lanesboro **American Legion** (103 Elmwood Street E., 1873) originally known as the Loveland Building, made of coursed asher stone and home to a millinery shop for decades. The Legion took it over in 1946. The **Lanesboro History Museum** (105 Parkway Ave. S.–1880), built by Michael Scanlan (and often called "Scanlan Hall"), housed various shops, second-floor apartments and a Chinese laundry in its basement. The **Lanesboro Creamery** (103 Coffee Street-1924) was home to the Lanesboro Co-Op Creamery that operated into the 1960s before its sale to Land O' Lakes. Dairy operations closed in 1973. Later the Scenic Valley Winery had a 25-year run selling its popular brand of wines, including "Rhubarb Wine" from here. **The DeVilliers building** (201 Parkway Ave. N.—about 1900), once known for confectionaries (and maybe a little moonshine), had upstairs living quarters for the DeVilliers family, while downstairs was, at various times, a restaurant, a vet office (around 1980), and a hair salon. Currently it's the Parkway Market and Coffee House.

In the early 1900s the **St. Mane Theater** on north Parkway Ave. was Manvel Olson's furniture store. He converted it into the Elite Theater to show silent movies. Later it was called the State Theater (1935) and featured piano playing from the balcony. It was also the first home of the Commonweal Theatre in the 1980s. Now owned by Lanesboro Arts, it currently hosts dozens of plays, concerts, films and "Over the Back Fence."

Church Hill

Saloons sprouted quickly in early Lanesboro. So did churches and schools. By 1869 the Presbyterians built a sanctuary on the high hill above the town's center. The Stone School House was constructed in 1870. Three years later St. Patrick's

Catholic Church opened its doors. In 1888 the Presbyterians—who had moved to a new location by the Mill Pond—sold their building to the Lutheran Church. The Lanesboro School was originally constructed in 1891.

Church Hill has seen a number major fires over the years. Determined town folk quickly rallied to rebuild their beloved structures, a tough task given the location. It makes you wonder: given those steep hills, not to mention icy Minnesota winters, why did early town folk decide to build on Church Hill? Two possibilities. First, sitting high above the river it avoided potential flooding. Second, the location offers a wonderful panoramic view of the town, the dam, the Root River, the entire valley. A view too good to miss, back then and still today.

"Brooklyn"

By the early 1870s the residential area south of Downtown was known as "Brooklyn," a nod to the founders' New York ties perhaps, or maybe because residents there had to contend with multiple river crossings. (The word "brooklyn" originally derived from the Dutch "breukelen" for "broken land," or German "bruoh," meaning "marshland."). A number of early downtown merchants built homes there when the Root River still flowed directly into Sylvan Park. In 1874 the river was re-directed, finally giving the residents of Brooklyn their first, direct Downtown access.

Brooklyn is blessed with wide streets, large lots, and many beautifully restored homes, a number of which are now B & Bs. One of Brooklyn's first homes was the James A. Thompson House (401 Parkway Avenue S., 1870), the brick Italianate residence of one of Lanesboro's original mill owners. The Scandinavian Inn (701 Kenilworth Avenue, 1892), built by Norwegian immigrant Ole Habberstad, co-owner of the Lanesboro Lumber Company, has a rooftop gazebo offering beautiful views of the town and bluffs. The Habberstad House Bed & Breakfast (706 Fillmore Avenue S., 1890) was built by Olaf and Celia Habberstad, owners of the Lanesboro Bank. Anna V's Bed & Breakfast (507 Fillmore Avenue S., 1908) was built by widow Anna Vickerman. The Vickerman's original Brooklyn home on the corner of Pleasant and Calhoun (1893), and built by Issac and Anna before his death, later became Dr. Johnson's "hospital." Other stately homes in Brooklyn include the Cady Hayes House (on the corner of Calhoun and Kirkwood, 1894), built by a retired farmer who greatly expanded the residence that became a B & B in the early 1990s, the Scanlan House (708 Parkway Ave. S, 1890), built by Michael Scanlan, was one of

In 1998 the National Trust for Historic Preservation granted Lanesboro its Great American Main Street Award.

the first homes in Lanesboro to have its own water system, with water piped from a hillside well high above it (site of the present-day Lanesboro Golf Course) to a large cistern in the home's basement. It is now the Historic Scanlan House Bed & Breakfast.

"Little Norway"

Lanesboro's prominent immigrant heritage remains alive in the name of a small contingent of houses and outbuildings located just to the west of the Bass Pond. A half-dozen or so still-occupied homes make up Little Norway today, with a small, wooden foot bridge providing access to the adjacent Root River State Trail.

"The Flat"

The Flat sits at the eastern edge of Lanesboro on the bank of the Root River. Trains traveled through this area of town, many homes were built here, and it was also the location for vital town businesses, including the lumberyard, a grain elevator, the cement block factory, and farther down, the still-operating Lanesboro Sales Barn.

Little Norway, 1900

A tunnel is said to exist under Coffee Street that connected the DeVillier Confectionary Store and Hanson Drug.

A Bike Ride on the Root River Trail

"The best thing about the Root River Trail is that it doesn't go in a straight line.
It curves along, parallel to the river, and always gives you
something different to look at."

Dave Harrenstein

It's a crystal-clear fall morning in Lanesboro, the temperature is around 70, and the sky is brilliant blue. A perfect day for a bike ride. Many—including me—consider this the best season for biking. Fall colors are nearing peak today, and crimson, green and gold leaves are bursting everywhere. I've lived in New England and I've seen Vermont's breathtaking October hillsides. Autumn in Minnesota's bluff country ranks right up there.

Even better, I get to enjoy all this on the Root River State Trail. I'm embarrassed to admit I lived in Lanesboro for more than a year before I took my first bike ride on this trail. What a mistake. It would be like living in Paris and not visiting the Louvre.

Lanesboro sits mid-point on this 60-mile paved trail, a well-maintained (thank you, DNR) asphalt ribbon that winds from Fountain to Houston, with extended trail-jogs to Preston and Harmony. I've heard many avid bikers say the Root River trail is one of the most enjoyable in Minnesota. Maybe even the entire Midwest. The combination of river and trail, of farm, field and forest, is almost—here's that Lanesboro word again—magical.

As we learned earlier, most of the Root River Trail is the abandoned railroad line of the Southern Minnesota (later the Milwaukee Road) Railroad. Today I'll ride one of its most popular sections, the 13 miles between Lanesboro and Peterson. There are good reasons why people love this part. The trail hugs the river most of the way with just a few slight hills, making it rider-friendly for all ages and biking levels. The fact that Whalan's Aroma Pie Shop is on the way doesn't hurt. Never underestimate the motivational power of rhubarb cream.

My ride begins on Coffee Street near the Post Office where the trail glides down and is swallowed into a grove of trees. The Lanesboro Sales Barn comes quickly on the right—you'll hear boisterous greetings from inside on most days—and soon I'm crossing a sturdy old railroad bridge with the Root River swirling below. I'm on my way.

The Root River is a tributary of the Upper Mississippi River and flows into the Mississippi River south of La Crosse, Wisconsin.

In less than a mile I reach the "confluence," where the North Root River and the South Root River merge. The river is low today and looks friendly, even serene. That's not always the case. After a hard rain the confluence is turbulent with rushing waters tearing into nearby banks, even uprooting trees. Crossing an-other railroad bridge, the highest in

Bobcat

the area, I look over to a sandy shoreline that on hot, summer days collects a con-gregation of dozens of tubers, canoers, and kayakers. Not today. These October wa-ters are chilly. I have this paradise to myself right now. No complaints.

I'm not totally alone. Birds are flitting, chirping and singing in the canopy of hardwood trees overhead. Wrens, finches, jays, all kinds of songbirds. I search branches to find my favorites, cardinals and indigo buntings. Hawks are common here. So are bald eagles. You'll often spot them soaring high above the river looking for fish. (Don't be fooled by those other high-flying birds, the numerous and much-less-majestic turkey vultures). On the edges of farms and fields—occasionally on the trail itself—you might come across wild turkeys, too, always skitterish, sometimes cranky. Best to keep pedaling and leave them be.

Deer are a pleasant and common site on these rides. Even on the trail sometimes. (All around Lanesboro actually—Susie's hosta patch is more salad bar than flower garden). Coming around a trail bend to find a doe and fawn calmly staring at you is one of those Lanesboro biking moments that keep people coming back here.

Bikers need to know that the limestone bluffs in this river valley are home to Min-nesota's largest population of timber rat-tlesnakes. Not as many as decades ago when

they were collected by the hundreds for bounties, but they're still around. This kind of weather—warm sunshine after a cool night—is when they often seek the warmth

Red Fox

of the black asphalt. A DNR naturalist once told me if he had to find a timber rattlesnake in Minnesota the first place he'd look would be under any of the small wooden bridges on the Root River trail between Lanesboro and Whalan. Again, just good to know. Nothing to fret over. If you do spot one—they're protected and shouldn't be disturbed—quickly pedal by. You'll both be happy. That goes for other snakes you might see along the way, like garter or bull snakes.

Heads up is always good advice on the trail, and not just for snakes. On summer days especially it can be a busy place with a fun mix of experienced riders, weekend warriors, and once-a-year-I-get-my-bike-out-of-the-garage bikers. Small kids on bikes are fun to watch but can be unpredictable. Staying on your right and calling out a cheerful "on your left" as you pass other bikers (and walkers) is important etiquette. Safety and courtesy make the trail work better for everyone.

"Always wear a bike helmet!" we advise our B & B guests. The smart ones listen. You may feel totally confident, but you just never know what might happen. Dave, a veteran biker from Duluth, returns each summer to enjoy the trail. He wears a helmet and that's a good thing. Last summer, while pedaling along peacefully towards Whalan, a large (apparently angry) bird flew directly into the side of his head. Startled, Dave fell off his bike and crashed into trailside bushes. A visit to Urgent Care in Rochester cleaned his scrapes and scratches, thankfully leaving him only a dented helmet, a few bruises, and a pretty good story.

White-tail Fawn and Doe

My leisurely pace brings me to Whalan in about 30 minutes. Passing the Gator Mini-Golf course and Treasures on the Trail gift shop on the left, I arrive at the center

A plan to extend the Root River State Trail from Harmony to the Niagara Cave and the Iowa border was proposed in 1989 and remains under active consideration.

of this small (population 63) but irresistible town. Whalan is proud home to the "Stand Still Parade" each May and a pie shop that's been helping bikers refuel and relax for a quarter century. All the pies are great. So is watching hummingbirds on the shop's feeders. I indulge in both today, and after a slice of French Silk, I'm back on the trail to burn off those calories.

I pass the scenic log cabins and expansive green lawns of Cedar Valley Resort and continue on towards Peterson. The farm fields are now cleared of corn but are still adorned with wild flowers. The DNR widened and re-paved this section of the trail last year. Nearly every year a section is upgraded and improved. People like this trail and take good care of it. Litter is rare. In winter the DNR also grooms the trail (after snowfalls of at least six inches) for cross-country skiing. Today's no time to think about that. Winter will come soon enough.

Timber Rattlesnake

Suddenly I lose the river as its bends off to the southeast and pass a few more iconic farm scenes with weathered red barns, small brick silos, and rolling fields stretching for miles. I reach Peterson (population 199), founded in 1853 by Peter Peterson Haslerud that has a fine museum, two B & Bs, Geneva's ice cream shop, and Burdey's Cafe, a friendly spot that also serves up excellent pie, tasty comfort food, and smiling people.

Regretfully I don't have room for more pie yet, so after a brief water stop, I turn my bike 180 degrees to begin the journey back to Lanesboro. I'm thankful for this good ride today. Every day on the trail is unique. Different weather, river conditions, animals, birds—you never know what you'll see. But you always know it will be worth it to get out here. You'll be eager to do it again. That's the solid promise of a day on the Root River Trail.

In September, 1874, a large black bear wandered into Lanesboro but was quickly shooed back into the woods.

A Breakfast at the Spud Boy Diner

'When I first saw this diner it was in terrible shape. After restoration, it's better than new. It's the little diner that died and went to heaven…I mean Lanesboro."
Gordon Tindall

The Spud Boy Diner is at 105 ¾ Parkway Avenue North, shoehorned into a cozy, 27-foot lot between Crown Trout Jewelers and the Amish Experience Gift Shop. Four grey metal steps lead up to its front door. That's a short climb but quite a journey. Time travel, really. All the way back to 1926.

That's when this diner was built by the Goodell Dining Car Company in Silver Creek, New York. Under various owners and names (Helen's Diner, The Village Diner, and Carl's Trackside Diner) it traveled from New York to Ohio to southeastern Minnesota before finding its perfect home.

Spud Boy is painted a creamy yellow and has white trim. It sits sturdily on four large wooden wheels that are lime-green. Darker green lettering on its sides tells you what to do and expect. "Eat Lunch." "Good Food." "Booth Service for Ladies." Come on in.

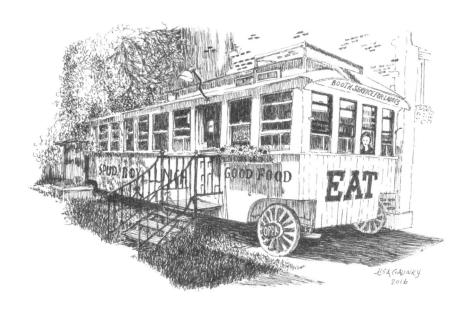

"You can't hide in a diner. Before you leave I guarantee you'll know the person sitting next to you." (Gordon Tindall)

When you do you find its owners, Gordie and Val Tindall, hard at work behind the counter. Gordie and Val opened Spud Boy here in May, 2012, and keep it open daily from May 1st to Halloween. Not easy work, but you can tell they love it.

Gordie is in his late 60s, a tall Lincolnesque figure with a shock of grey hair. A retired railroad worker, he loves old things: 1860s baseball, pool halls (he's putting one of those in Lanesboro, too), and especially old diners. His renovation of Spud Boy was his third diner "rescue."

What does he like about diners? "Everything," Gordie says. "The way they look. The way they feel. I like eating in them. I like working in them. A diner brings people together. It's a very human place."

Years ago Gordie was operating the Red Rose Diner in Towanda, Pennsylvania, when a friend asked if he might have interest in another old diner destined for demolition. "Its windows were boarded, the floor was warped, the paint was peeling," he remembers. "I saw all that, but I saw potential, too. So I told him yes." Over the next six years his thousands of hours of repair work brought the 10' by 30' rectangular diner back to life and he christened it "Spud Boy," a nickname he got from boyhood friends watching him haul potatoes on his father's farm near Dutch Neck, New Jersey.

On a fall morning Susie and I walk up those four steps to see what's cooking at Spud Boy. The place is busy and full of chatter, a mix of bluff country leaf-peepers and Lanesboro locals. Not quite capacity (that would be 20) but happily full.

"Sit anywhere you'd like," the waitress cheerfully instructs us. "All seats are equally uncomfortable." We choose two of the dozen round stools facing the grill. I watch knees get bumped as two couples squeeze into one of the two front booths. People must have been smaller in 1926. No one seems to mind, though. Cozy is the unofficial theme of the Spud Boy Diner.

The smell of hot coffee warms the place. Gordie—sporting bushy mutton chop sideburns today for his current turn in the Lanesboro Community Theater production of "Mary Poppins"—is at the grill. Val, wearing a vintage-flowered apron and a nifty black beret, is also busy, scribbling orders on a palm-sized note pad.

Gordie starts that coffee about 5:30 each morning. Val arrives soon after and the two commence their diner dance (the Spud Boy Shuffle?), constantly squeezing by each other in the tight quarters between counter and grill. If they weren't already happily married, you think they'd want or need to be. It all seems to work.

In 1988 the Lanesboro School became the first school in Minnesota to open a Day Care Center.

The menu is straight-forward and encouraging. "Order with confidence," it says. "We take pride in what we serve. Everything's pretty good here." Susie and I have been here before. We know the food—classic breakfast fare—is good. So are the prices—eggs over easy, hash browns, toast, some of that coffee, will run about $7. Cash or check only, please.

While I wait for my food I watch Gordie slide a large pie out of an old Roper Stove. He makes one pie a day from scratch. This one is apples and blueberries under a crumbly brown sugar topping. He places it on the counter to cool, aware of my lustful glance. "Not ready until lunch today," he tells me with a smile. What makes a good pie, I ask? "Lard," he answers firmly. "But sometimes that can have a barnyard smell, so I use Crisco® more often these days."

Look around Spud Boy's interior and you'll appreciate Gordie's craftsmanship and attention to detail. The varnished wood panel walls and ceiling have a reddish shine. The linoleum floor is worn but clean. High rectangular windows coax in an autumn morning breeze and the antique wall clock tells you to "Drink O-So-Grape Soda!" You're back in a long-ago American era when thousands of diners like this, in towns big and small, served simple, good, affordable food. Very few are left, just a handful are as old as Spud Boy.

Gordie restored this diner with period equipment. All of its vintage appliances still work, too, including the potato slicer, the coffee grinder, the Frigidaire refrigerator, and that Roper Stove. That means we're smelling and tasting the same kind of good food people were enjoying almost 90 years ago. Lucky them. Lucky us.

Gordie is especially proud of his grill. "I found that in Syracuse—it's at least a 100 years old. When a grill gets seasoned like that over time, well, it just makes food taste better."

The man on the stool next to Susie begins describing in some detail his recent Twin Cities hospital stay. Gordie, his back turned as he's frying eggs is still able to listen and offers his own prescription. "You just need some good diner food is all." He sets my plate in front of me. "I broke one of the eggs, you get an extra," he tells me. The food here is local and fresh. "Do today's customers ask for vegan or gluten-free?" I ask. Gordie shrugs. "We don't think about that stuff here," he says. "Doesn't come up much."

Lanesboro's population in 1917 was about 1,000.

He scans Val's next written order with a hint of a scowl. Another egg problem. "Just says 'scram,'" he calls to her. "How many?" "One," she answers. Small talk fits close quarters.

I get a chance to ask Val how business is faring these days. "We judge that by the number of maple syrup jugs we use," she says. "This season we're on number eight. Not great, not bad." Each winter they discuss Spud Boy economics and future plans. "We take it year by year," Gordie says.

Hopefully those maple jugs will keep flowing. Everyone blessed enough to walk the four steps into this place—Lanesboro locals and bluff country tourist alike—is in for a rare treat. You go back in time, rub shoulders with old and new friends, and enjoy a great breakfast at a fair price. All of that and coffee, too. What a bargain. See you tomorrow, Gordie, for a piece of that pie.

Flour Mill and railroad spur

The Lanesboro History Museum displays Purple Hearts awarded to local military heroes: Lester Hatleli (World War II), Paul Hildestad (Korea) and Richard Overland (Vietnam).

A Morning at the Sales Barn

"What can you smell before you see it and hear before you smell it?"

The Lanesboro Sales Commission, of course, commonly called the Sales Barn. If you don't count the bank building on the corner of Parkway and Coffee that's had multiple owners and names, the Sales Barn is currently the longest-running business in Lanesboro. It's also a business whose impact far eclipses those noises and smells. This business makes a difference to the entire state.

The Sales Barn is located on the southeast corner of the Flat off Coffee Street, adjacent to the Highway 250 Campground, a slightly disjointed collection of multi-sized grey pole barns, sheds and animal pens. It sits at the base of a towering limestone bluff, tucked between the South Branch of the Root River and the Root River State Trail. It can be a little tough to find, but not for the farmers, cattle men and livestock breeders who've been coming here weekly for auctions since 1947.

That's the year the Sales Commission was started by Paul Evenson, Water Ode, and Duffy Lewis. The Joe Nelson family purchased it in 1994 and continues to run it today. The tradition continues and gets passed along, with three and four generation families still selling and buying livestock here at the weekly auctions.

I see more cattle trucks on Lanesboro's main street than school busses, so I'm aware of the Sales Barn. I'm also one of those who doesn't really know what they actually do there. Only one way to find out. On a Friday morning in May, I decide to follow one of those big trucks to find out for myself.

I'm nervous about this. Not sure why. I spent summers as a kid on my Grampa's small farm in Utah. I did chores, milked cows, fed chickens, hauled hay. But this feels different, kind of like the major leagues of farm and cattle stuff. As I pull into the Sales Barn's unpaved parking lot, a mess of slippery mud this morning after an overnight rain, I park my Toyota Highlander. I feel out of place. This is a parking lot for trucks. Heavy duty trucks. The kind Sam Elliot growls about. And livestock trailers. I do see two Amish buggies and horses tied to nearby trees. That helps a bit, although I'm not sure why. At least they aren't trucks.

In 1873 a brewery near the site of the present-day Sales Barn made "Lanesboro Brand Beer" before closing six years later.

I park and quickly slink towards the buildings. My immediate goal is to just blend in. Good luck with that. The guys getting out of those big trucks are wearing denim work shirts, jeans, bib overalls with fresh farm muck, cowboy hats and feed-store caps. I'm wearing jeans, too. But with a yellow golf shirt and tennis shoes. Bad choice, I'm thinking. And I'm carrying a clipboard. Geez.

I don't speak from experience here, but this must be what it feels like to walk into a strip club for the first time. I feel awkward, out of place. I don't know where to go or where to sit. I have fuzzy notions about what goes on in here, but no specifics. My forehead and palms are getting sweaty. All the other guys (you can tell they've been here before) look confident, relaxed, almost smug. They know exactly what's going to happen. Is it just me, or are people staring at me? Must be the clipboard. Just keep walking, Steve.

I open the door to the Stockyard Café. I know that's what it is because it has a red neon-sign outline of a cow on the front and the word Café. Small groups of men sit on folding chairs drinking coffee, eating donuts, talking loud. I smile and nod a greeting aimed at no one in particular. Lanesboro is a friendly town, but some places definitely cater to locals. This is one of them. A few guys glance at me and their eyes narrow. I see a hallway leading to a large barn and quickly head for it. Turns out I'll see a lot of that kind of activity this morning.

I do know I'm going to see a live animal auction. Some are here to sell lambs, goats, calves, and cows. Others are here to buy them. Their transactions help both parties, obviously, but the prices paid today will also help set current prices for those animals across southern Minnesota. It's important stuff. I sense the people here know what they're doing. It looks like a few of them have been doing it for a very long time.

The center of attention in the main Sales Barn is a large rectangular pen about the size of a skinny tennis court, sunken between two sets of steep bleachers that face each other. It has the look and feel of a 1950s high school basketball gym. (It even smells a bit like that, if memory serves). Perched high above everything on the far end, in a booth crowded with desks and computer screens, are two people who will run this show: the auctioneer and a lady on a telephone.

I glance around and see the kinds of people I'd expected to see. A couple of dozen men, a few women, farmers, ranchers, cattle men, I'm thinking. A middle-aged to older crowd although a few younger couples find bleacher seats, too. Some women hold babies on their laps or tend small children. A few of the oldest-looking guys climb the tall bleacher steps in slow motion, greeting friends on their way up like you'd hear in a neighborhood bar. I wonder if they're here to actually buy anything or just for the coffee, donuts, and teasing chatter with their buddies about cows, beef prices and weather. A handful of Amish men in blue shirts and straw hats are here, too. The guys with the buggies, I figure.

The action begins when a large door swings open on the far end of the pen and about ten bleating small lambs trot out, guided by two men using long, whippy, flagged poles to move them along. The auctioneer, talking amazingly fast like only auctioneers can do, calls for bids, bids are made and in about 30 seconds, the first auction is already over. The big swinging door opens again, the handlers quickly herd the lambs back out, the swinging gate-door slams behind them. Weights and price numbers get announced and immediately flash on large TV monitors sitting high on both ends of the barn.

The lady next to the auctioneer is busy talking on her phone. I learn from the man sitting next to me (a friendly farmer from Cresco, Iowa) that people are making on-line bids, too. Much is happening here in a very short time frame. It all happens smoothly, quickly. Very impressive.

The auction gains momentum. Those first lambs are followed by groups of goats, calves, and sheep herded through what must be a maze of connected chutes. The auctioneer breathlessly runs through the inventory, occasionally adding bits of color commentary. "Look at that calf," he says. "Talk about a nice one." Goats appear next. "That's one a fine nanny," he says. "Giving two gallons of milk a day." He knows these animals personally or he's working off good notes, I'm guessing. More animals trot in, handlers move them along, bids are made, animals get sold, gate opens, slams shut, get sold, numbers flash, next!

I know bleacher-people are making bids. Darned if I can figure out how. I don't hear anybody saying anything. Trying not to be rude, I stare intently at the people sitting around me, trying to catch their "signals." It must be slight nods and quick hand-gestures. Then I start to worry that one wrong twitch on my part or an ill-timed sneeze will have me going home with a goat. Or worse. I sit very still and hang tight to my clipboard.

"Over the Back Fence" did its first show in 1995 for Valentine's Day and soon became a weekly live radio show on KFIL.

"You bring your homework today?" asks the friendly farmer in bib overalls from Spring Valley sitting behind me. "No, just trying to figure things out here," I answer. "Well, you've got buyers and sellers," he tells me with a smile. "That's pretty much it."

Watching this fast-moving, choreographed action, my mind shifts gears from a strip club motif to the fancy dog shows you see on TV each February. Lots of similarities. Excited animals prancing around, people leaning forward, staring at them with great interest. High-speed judging. A similar winner/loser atmosphere, too. Mooing, no barking, though. All fast-paced, moving quickly to a conclusion.

About 20 minutes into the action, some late-comers approach the bleachers. No overalls or manure-stained boots in this group. It's three women in their late 50's in floral dresses carrying large purses. They're chatting, laughing, giggling even as they struggle up the tall steep bleacher steps. All three seem excited to be here. They sit near enough to me that I can politely ask a question or two while we're waiting for the next animal group. "Is this your first visit to the Sales Barn?" I ask, acting like it isn't mine. "Oh, we've never been here before," answers the friendly lady with highly-piled, slightly pinkish hair. "We're sisters. We live near Rushford. We've always wondered what happens here. My sister, Helen, says it's been on her bucket list to visit the Sales Barn. It was raining today and we didn't feel like shopping, so here we are! We want to see some animals before we get pie in Whalan."

They're in luck. Groups of animals just keep coming. After watching a half dozen calves from Caledonia come and go, I figure I've seen enough, grab my clip board, and step down the bleachers. The last thing I hear as I hit the door is the bleating of another group of lambs and excited giggles from the Rushford sisters. A fitting end to a fun morning at the Lanesboro Sales Commission. My first visit, hopefully not my last. This belongs on people's bucket lists, I'd say. Maybe next time, since I'm no longer a rookie, I'll come a little early. Maybe even try one of those donuts.

The Lanesboro Creamery produced 350,000 pounds of butter in 1938.

A Visit to the Fish Hatchery

"It's great having the hatchery in Lanesboro. It brings the right
people here who know how to manage fish."
Steve Sobieniak, The Root River Rod Co.

Lanesboro's biggest fish story starts a mile south of town off Grosbreak Road at the site of a geological wonder most people don't even know about. They should, especially people who like to fish. In Minnesota that's a lot of people.

We're talking about the Duschee Mill Spring, a natural flowing artesian spring where crystal-clear water gushes like a firehose directly out of a rocky hillside, 24/7,

365 days a year. When first measured a century ago, nearly 10,000 gallons of water poured from the spring every minute. It's down to a still impressive 5,000 gallons a minute and is one of the largest spring flows in the entire state.

Why should fishermen care about this? Because the Duschee Mill Spring is also site of the Lanesboro Fish Hatchery, the largest of four cold water fish hatcheries in Minnesota. What happens here has a huge impact on fish populations (and how many fish are caught) across the entire state.

The original name of the Fish Hatchery was the "Root River Basin Trout Hatchery."

The spring is here because of Lanesboro's unique karst geology with its complex system of caves, sinkholes, springs, and subterranean streams. The water flowing out of this hillside is a sign of that. Combine that water with the acidic nature of local limestone rock and you have a perfect breeding environment for certain types of small flies and aquatic insects that fish love to eat. All of this makes Lanesboro—this entire region—a trout fisherman's paradise.

Rainbow Trout

The Duschee Mill Spring has been gushing water for hundreds, perhaps thousands of years. Excavation work for hatchery ponds in the 1920s discovered Native American relics, proof that people visited this spring, perhaps even lived near it, long ago. In the late 1800s Lanesboro settlers found it, too. Ole Duschee bought the land in 1876 and used the spring's gushing water to power his flour mill. He later abandoned the mill but his name remains.

Why is the hatchery here? That story begins in the early 1900s with unhappy local fishermen who had plenty of great fishing spots (there are over 700 miles of spring creeks in southeastern Minnesota) but who weren't catching many fish. Blame was pointed at farming practices like field run-off that raised water temperatures and were harming spawning and hatching conditions. Farmers responded and improvements were made. But people still wondered about other ways to increase fish populations.

In the 1920s naturalists working for the forerunner to the Minnesota Department of Natural Resources (DNR) theorized that Duschee Spring's constant flow of clean, well-oxygenated water with a steady year-round temperature of 48 degrees might create a natural "nursery" for raising fish. In 1925 the state purchased 18 acres of the old mill site for $11,000 and used its abandoned equipment to construct a hatchery. Their first attempt in 1926 failed, but the next year they produced a hatch of nearly 300,000 brook trout. The Lanesboro Hatchery has been helping keep fishermen happy ever since.

The state later purchased an additional 130 acres of nearby land. In the 1930s WPA workers expanded hatchery ponds and raceways and built housing for hatchery workers. In 1952 a large fire destroyed the site's main buildings, but they were replaced within two years. In 1956 more land was purchased that included a second, smaller spring ½ mile upstream. In 1985 28 more acres were added.

Today the Lanesboro Fish Hatchery has 56 fiberglass fry troughs for hatching fish and 56 fiberglass super troughs for fingerlings. It also has six outdoor earthen rearing ponds with 34 concrete raceways of various sizes for fingerling, yearling and brood stock production. All of that combines to give the Lanesboro Hatchery an incubator capacity of 2.4 million trout eggs that produce more than 700,000 rainbow and brown trout each year.

Stream trout don't reproduce in lakes; annual stocking is the only way to maintain those fish populations state-wide. The Lanesboro Hatchery provides nearly 98% of all trout fingerlings in Minnesota streams. It's also responsible for stocking more than 100 Minnesota lakes, from the Twin Cities to Baudette, Montrose, Bemidji, Park Rapids, Hutchinson, Detroit Lakes, Brainerd, Duluth, Grand Marais, and Ely.

Here's how it works. During spawning season (October through December) trout eggs are gathered from captive brood stocks. The eggs hatch and the fish are grown to either fingerling stage (by spring or fall of their first year) or to yearling size (by spring of their second year). At that point they can be transported for stocking.

The hatchery is open to the public on weekdays; self-guiding tour brochures and video displays are available. Visitors can see the spring, the ponds and the troughs. Feeding buckets are often available next to the ponds—throw in the fish-food pellets and you'll see pond-waters erupt with the bubbling frenzy of 170,000 young rainbow trout fingerlings.

You can't fish at the Hatchery but there are fishing spots—including seven accessible locations—on Duschee Creek as it flows away from the Hatchery. A hiking trail by the creek offers interpretive signs and is open year-round.

If Lanesboro is a series of simple pleasures, watching cool, clear, fresh water flowing non-stop from a green moss-covered hillside may be one of the simplest and prettiest of all. And one that should make fishermen across our state very happy indeed.

Legends say the Jesse James Gang camped south of Lanesboro (near today's Fish Hatchery) before their fateful bank robbery in Northfield on September 7, 1876.

A Trip to Avian Acres

"I love watching birds. Turns out most people do."

Bob Thomas, Avian Acres

Bird-watching is hugely popular in this country. And it keeps growing. About 11 million people watched the Daytona 500 on TV this year. 23 million follow baseball. 24 million are into basketball. NFL games average around 30 million viewers. How many birders are there? The Fish & Wildlife Service estimates 47 million.

Both casual bird watchers and enthusiastic birders enjoy visiting Avian Acres in Lanesboro. Getting there can create a few white knuckles, but it's worth the trip. You'll meet Bob Thomas there, Avian Acres' creator, owner and soul-force, a man with a passion for birds. He knows birds, feeds birds, studies birds. And he'll gladly tell you about them.

Avian Acres is at 32637 Grit Road on a high bluff two miles west of town, just off Oxcart Trail, an historic road with hairpin turns that work best when only one car at a time uses them. When two try, especially if one's a truck, it can get tricky. That's where the white knuckles come in, but friendly negotiations make it all work.

Bluejay

I took that road on a recent summer morning to meet Bob and learn about Avian Acres. In his early 60's, he has short, gray hair and a friendly, but firm, air. He greets me mop in hand because a thunderstorm dumped two inches of water into his barn-store overnight and he's spent the morning cleaning up. He waves me towards a seat on the front porch. His weary eyes suddenly spring to life. We're going to talk about birds.

Bob is an Army vet whose military family moved often when he was growing up. Their longest stay was in Hudson, Wisconsin, where at age seven he discovered birds. "My Grampa taught me to identify a white-breasted nuthatch," he remembers. "He called it the upside-down bird. That hooked me."

The South Branch of the Root River disappears underground and re-emerges later near the Mystery Cave near Preston.

Years later Bob and his wife visited Lanesboro from their Twin Cities home on a whim (we've heard that one before), found a piece of land they couldn't resist, and by 1993 "Avian Acres—Your Backyard Birding Headquarters" was open for business.

Why here? Few places in Minnesota are better for birding than bluff country, Bob tells me. Avian Acres, with 20 acres of thick forest and an historic 1911 dairy barn, attracts scores of bird species, including finches, woodpeckers (hairy, downy and pileated), flickers, jays, cardinals, orioles, bluebirds, eastern feebees, hummingbirds, starlings, sapsuckers, robins, nut hatches, indigo buntings,

Indigo Bunting

cuckoos, rose-breasted grosbeaks, crows, brown creepers, blackbirds, cowbirds, common sparrows, Canada geese, tufted titmice, summer and scarlet tanangers, hawks, owls, wild turkeys, and more. Eagles and turkey vultures soar overhead. For a while Bob even had some peacocks.

Cardinal

When Bob bought this property he didn't really have a plan for it. "I tried truck farming at first," he says. "Sold raspberries and asparagus. Birds and varmints caused too many problems so I got chickens and sold eggs. That was slow so I took a job in Rochester at a bird seed store. When that store closed I didn't know what I was going to do."

When leaving the store, Bob taped his phone number to the front door in case anyone needed bird seed. "A few months later a lady from Winnipeg called," Bob says. "She told me her father was in a Chatfield nursing home and asked if I'd keep his bird feeder full. I said sure.

"Earlier a feed-store friend had suggested I try selling bird seed from Lanesboro. Then I drove by a sign in Rochester for a restaurant called 'The Aviary,' a word that means a large area where birds are

Nuthatch

The Lanesboro School on Church Hill has been transformed into condominiums.

kept. I loved birds. I had a great place for a birder-support business. It all came together. Avian Acres."

Bob experimented with different seeds, soon developed 13 custom mixes for attracting specific birds, and began handing out "Bob's Mix" samples around Fillmore County. Orders soon began coming in. Today he has a customer data base of more than 13,000 names and he supplies bird seed to hundreds of regular customers. He personally delivers orders in 17 counties in Minnesota and

Bumble-bee

western Wisconsin. Hundreds of people also make that Oxcart Trail drive each year to visit Avian Acres, buy seed, feeders and other birder merchandise, do some birdwatching, and soak up Bob's love for birds.

"Southeastern Minnesota and the Root River Valley attracts birds and birders," Bob explains. "This is north-south migratory corridor is part of the Mississippi River basin. Thousands of birds fly through here each spring and fall and put on a real show."

Bob has identified more than 200 different types of birds at Avian Acres. "People ask me what's the rarest bird I've seen," he says. "The yellow-billed cuckoo. Saw it once, maybe twice. That's what makes birding fun—you never know what you'll see or when. I identify birds by their calls, too. The best way to pick out warblers, for example, is by their unique songs."

Bob talks fast. Pay attention and you learn a lot. "Birds are visual," he says. "No sense of smell. No sweat glands in their feet, either. They can walk on ice and snow which helps in Minnesota. Gold finches like a crowd. Not cardinals. Give them lots of space. The key with all birds is be quiet, watch, listen."

Are birds like people, I ask? "In many ways, yes," Bob says. "Some are colorful; some are ordinary. Some are bullies; some are timid. Some like company; others are loners. Take blue jays. They're the most controversial backyard bird. They're bold and dramatic. They fly in loud and blind. 'Here I am. Deal with me!' Some people are like that, too."

Bob loves birds. He also loves helping other people enjoy them. "Birds are amazing creatures. They can fly. I can't fly. They can sing. I can't sing. Birds are a special part of God's creation. It's wonderful that we can enjoy all of that right here in Lanesboro."

The Farmers and Merchants Lumber Company was located at the northeast section of town near the Flat for more than a century.

A Ride on an Amish Tour

"Lutherans believe in the Ten Commandments and are very careful about most of them. The Amish are serious about all 10."

A black horse pulls a covered buggy up Parkway Avenue's gentle slope near the Lanesboro Dam. In a nearby parking lot a bearded man in a blue shirt and straw hat and a woman in a plain brown dress and white bonnet stand at a table selling quilts, woven baskets, and honey. Who are they? That's easy. They're Amish. Why are we so curious about them? That's harder to answer.

American popular culture can't get enough of the Amish. The 1985 movie "Witness" starring Harrison Ford released an avalanche of Amish-themed movies, plays, and books. (In a recent year twenty-three series of Amish romance novels were published). Weird Al's "Amish Paradise" parody has 50 million YouTube hits. Reality TV shows like "Breaking Amish," "Amish Mafia," and "Amish Haunting" have strange names—and millions of fans.

The Amish get their name from Anabaptists who followed the teachings of Jakob Ammann in the late 1600's.

Many take their curiosity a step further and visit Amish country. Lancaster County, Pennsylvania, is the epicenter for that, but the Midwest has similar places like Kalona, Iowa, Cashton, Wisconsin—and Lanesboro, Minnesota.

We live in Lanesboro and see Amish folks regularly. We hire Amish workers at our B & B. We enjoy visits with nice people like Dan Gingerich, Moses Miller, and Sam Swartzentruber. We admire Amish hand-crafted furniture and enjoy their homemade treats (the chocolate cashew crunch is addicting). The clip-clop of their horses on local streets is familiar and soothing.

I'm curious about the Amish, too. Luckily my neighbor, Vern, a retired computer programmer who looks like a professor has the smarts of one when it comes to all-things Amish. He's been an Amish tour guide and "driver" for nearly a decade. I arrange a tour with him one fall morning and start with the basics. Who are the Amish, when did they come to bluff country, and why do they live such "simple" lives?

"The Amish are German in heritage," Vern tells me. "A group of families arrived in Fillmore County in the mid-1970s from Ohio to buy land, start farms, and raise their children. About 700 live here now, mostly near Canton, Mabel, Harmony and Lanesboro."

Approximately 300,000 Amish live in 38 states with the largest concentrations in Pennsylvania, Ohio, Indiana, Wisconsin, Minnesota, Iowa, and Kansas. "The Amish are united by their deep commitment to faith and family," says Vern. "They live out that commitment in a rural lifestyle guided by their local church."

Amish homes don't have electricity. No lights, TVs, computers, or appliances. No running water, either. Phone use is strictly limited. Dress and grooming is plain and identical, down to the buttons on their clothes. Married men have beards, no mustaches. Women don't wear make-up. Head coverings are required, even for children. Amish don't own or drive cars. They use horse-drawn buggies or hire non-Amish ("English," they call them) drivers for transportation. Train travel is okay. Airplanes are not. Farm work is manual, with some diesel generators and lots of (literal) horse power.

Their culture is rooted in the history and theology of the Protestant Reformation of the 1500s, but the Industrial Revolution three centuries later initiated the more conservative Amish lifestyle. "In the mid-1800s young men were leaving farms to work in cities," says Vern. "The Amish worried that urban temptations would harm their families and communities. A small segment felt so threatened they rejected the continuance of progress and drew a line in the sand at around 1860 as to what would be allowed and what wouldn't."

The Amish organize their communities into church districts of about 20 families each. They hold home-based services twice a month for worship, instruction and shared meals. A bishop leads the district and sees that the rules (or "ordnung") are followed. Those rules govern all matters of life: how to dress, what to eat, where to work, how children are educated, rituals for marrying and burying, and so on.

"Amish sing off the same page," says Vern. "They believe conformity creates harmony, while individuality risks pride, jealousy, and division. Nothing is more important to them than unity, and they follow their rules to achieve that."

I try to imagine life in an Amish home. No TVs. No computers. How do they relax at day's end, I ask? "They actually have conversations," Vern says with a smile. "Can you imagine that? They also read. Walk into an Amish home that has ten children and the first thing you'll notice is how quiet it is."

To us "English" that might seem strict and stifling. But Amish families choose this lifestyle, following in the footsteps of their parents, grandparents, and great-grandparents. They hope and expect their own children and grandchildren will choose that same path for generations to come.

Amish children can join the church at age 16 after a season of "rumspringa," a German word loosely translated as "running around," to help them decide. Most young people make their decision by age 18. About 85% of them remain Amish. If they decide not to join the church, they're no longer considered Amish. If Amish become "worldly" by defying local rules, they can be shunned, even expelled, at any age. "Lifestyle infractions—big or small—always result in discipline," says Vern. "That might be for a minor infraction like wearing a Twins baseball cap or something much worse. It all depends on the bishop and local church orders."

Amish children speak German (or "Pennsylvania Dutch") before learning English. They attend one-room Amish schools through the 8th grade then learn trades in their family or community business. Amish marriages aren't arranged but usually happen by their late teens or early 20s. "Even without movies, football games or dances, Amish young people still meet, fall in love and have the same romantic entanglements we all have," Vern says. "Non-Amish kids probably wonder how that's possible. But it is."

Many Amish farms near Lanesboro welcome "English" into their shops to purchase quilts, baskets, furniture, gift items, bakery goods and fresh produce. (No Sunday sales

Padding and helmets used by players on the Lanesboro High School football team in the early 1900s were made by local harness makers.

and no pictures, please). Amish merchants also sell goods in downtown Lanesboro where tours and self-guiding CDs are readily available.

My tour with Vern ends. My big question lingers. Why are we so curious about the Amish? "Their religion interests many," Vern says. "Others are fascinated by their lifestyle. In the last few years, though, I've noticed deeper, more personal reasons. Many people today feel overwhelmed by how busy life is. Family calendars are jammed. Cell phones keep ringing. The Amish world seems quieter, better balanced. People are drawn to that, I think."

I remember his words a few weeks later as I drive back to Lanesboro from Harmony after a long, errand-filled day. I'm tired and eager to get home. So eager I barely notice an orange-tinted full harvest moon balanced on the horizon. Coming around a corner on Highway 52 I hit my brakes to slow for an Amish buggy in front of me. My teeth clench, my hands tightly squeeze the steering wheel. "Finally!" I mutter when the buggy pulls off towards a dirt road, and I stab again at the gas pedal.

Then—and I'm not sure why—I take my foot off the gas. I slow down. I pause to watch that horse and buggy travel that dirt road, its two back wheels billowing a clouds of tan dust into a sky now pastel purple and maroon. Grey smoke is swirling from the chimney of the simple, white wood-frame house at the end of that road. I'm picturing the quiet evening ahead in that Amish home, already lit by candlelight, and I feel a strange tug. I'd like to follow that buggy, relax by that fire, soak in that quiet. I won't, of course. That's their world, not mine. I hit the gas pedal again and drive on. But I know I have things to learn from my Amish neighbors. I hope I'm wise enough to do just that.

Local dairy farming got an early boost in 1920 when 35 cows from Wisconsin—the first full-blooded Holsteins in the area—were delivered and sold to farmers by a local bank.

A Hike at Eagle Bluff

"The best way to learn about the environment is to be in the environment."
Joe Deden

On a beautiful May morning I'm going go for a hike. The trail I'll take is located three miles north of Lanesboro off County Road 8 and offers panoramic, top-of-the-bluff views of the Root River Valley. This seems like another hidden treasure, too, until you learn that nearly 17,000 people come here every year to enjoy this place. I'm at the Eagle Bluff Environmental Learning Center. There's nothing else quite like it anywhere in southern Minnesota.

The Eagle Bluff story was built on a dream with a side order of mushrooms. That all started in 1978 when Joe Deden, a forester who'd grown up near Red Wing, Minnesota, traveled to Germany to study different methods of environmental education. Joe worked with young students outdoors during the day while at night the young people stayed in hostels. He returned home wondering, "could a similar learning model work in Minnesota?"

Joe rallied a small group of like-minded folks to consider that idea and by 1980 their "Root River Hardwood Forest Interpretive Center" was offering adult education classes out of his basement. A new name—the "Southeast Minnesota Forest Resource Center"—and a partnership with the University of Minnesota's College of Natural Resources soon led them help landowners maximize the use of local forest lands through sustainable cash crops.

That's where those mushrooms come in, shitakes specifically, a popular edible mushroom native to East Asia. The Forest Resource Center discovered that hardwood logs in southeastern Minnesota work well for cultivating shitakes commercially. Before long Joe and his team were national leaders in that market.

His original vision—to help young people learn about the environment in outdoor settings—hadn't dimmed. Generous donations provided land and buildings near Lanesboro to create an on-site day-camp. Dorms and a dining hall were later added, opening the door to multiple-day and year-round use. In 1996 the newly-christened Eagle Bluff Environmental Learning Center welcomed its first overnight students.

More than a half-million students have benefited from the Eagle Bluff Learning Center in the past three decades.

Today Eagle Bluff, located on 250-acres, is a fully-accredited, non-profit, 250-bed residential environmental learning center, one of six in the Minnesota, and the second-largest next to Wolf Ridge Environmental Learning Center in Finland, Minnesota. More than 12,000 K-12 students from 135 different schools travel to Eagle Bluff each year (mostly from Minnesota, Iowa and Wisconsin) to participate in formal 3-5 day learning sessions. Two dozen staff members and a team of graduate-level naturalists guide students in their study of the environment, native plant and animal life, sustainable living practices, and conservation. Students also do high ropes courses (there are three levels of courses on-site), scale an indoor climbing wall, learn archery, take night hikes, go canoeing, and more. There are also summer camp options at Eagle Bluff.

Another 5,000 older students and adults also come to Eagle Bluff annually for environmental classes, staff-building retreats, family reunions, even a few weddings. Eleven miles of hiking trails, like the one I'm on today, and the ropes courses are open to the public. During the winter, cross-country skiing and snowshoeing are popular Eagle Bluff activities.

Eagle Bluff now offers Skills School, too, where adults learn new skills in hands-on classes like Orienteering, Dutch Oven Cooking, Fossil Hunting, Music for Wellness, Spey Casting and Raku Firing. The most popular class so far? Amish cooking.

The newest venture at Eagle Bluff is development of "The Point," a 150-acre hard-wood forest recently acquired from the Allen Gavere estate, described by Steve Klotz of Minnesota's DNR, as "...the most diverse, remote and fascinating piece of property left in the Root River watershed." EBLC will use the property to expand junior and senior high programs.

Eagle Bluff is growing strong connections to the wider Lanesboro community. Its staff live, work and play locally. A few have even served on non-profit boards. The connections go both ways. Volunteers from Lanesboro and other nearby towns put their expertise to work, like the Skills School cheese-making class taught by a Lanesboro man who made cheese at the Lanesboro Creamery for thirty years. Local friends take advantage of special Eagle Bluff programs like Dinner on the Bluff, Haunted High Ropes in October, and July's Monarch Butterfly Festival.

The forested trails at Eagle Bluff offer expansive views at almost every turn. At the hillside below the first overlook you'll see the remaining stone-foundation of the Root River Power and Light Company—and its 1,800 foot tunnel carved through limestone bluffs—that harnessed water power to provide electricity for eight local communities from 1912 to 1928. A fascinating story, certainly new to me.

The man-made stuff here is interesting. The natural scenic beauty, and its abundant bird and animal life, is awesome. Eagle Bluff—its name fits—is a birder's paradise. Eagles regularly soar overhead and scores of other types of birds migrate through and nest here. Bring your binoculars.

On my visit and hike, I learned much about Eagle Bluff and how this place enriches people of all ages through classes and innovative programs. Mostly what I take away, though, is a lasting reminder of how powerfully refreshing it is to spend time in nature. To see the big sky of bluff country. Smell a forest. Delight in the sights and sounds of calling birds. To stand still before the calming force of a flowing river.

Maybe all of that was in Joe Deden's dream. Thankfully for so many, hopefully for years to come, it's a dream that keeps coming true.

The Director's residence at Eagle Bluff Learning Center is only the ninth home in North America to achieve the Home Challenge (at least a 70% energy reduction).

An Evening with the Rhubarb Sisters

"Rhubarb is a metaphor for finding happiness in your own backyard."

Peggy Hanson

Lanesboro has a love affair with rhubarb. That may sound strange, but it makes perfect sense here. There's something about this sour, reddish-green vegetable (fruit?) with the funny name that captures the spirit of this place. That became official in 2008 when Lanesboro was named Minnesota's official Rhubarb Capital. Can't argue with the government.

On a warm June evening I'm headed to a concert at the St. Mane Theater headlined by the Rhubarb Sisters, four ladies in pink high-top Converse tennis-shoes, vintage house dresses and non-matching aprons, who, in various configurations, have been celebrating rhubarb in song and style for more than a decade. This concert will cap another Rhubarb Festival, a day-long event held in Sylvan Park the first Saturday of June. If you really want to discover the essence of Lanesboro, this day ties it all together and puts a bow on it. A reddish-green, of course.

Before we take our seat, let's cover rhubarb basics. First, it is a vegetable that works as a fruit. It sprouts large green leaves, some as big as an elephant's ear (which happen to be poisonous—the leaves, not the ears), and has firm reddish, green, pink, crimson, even speckled stalks. It comes in many varieties (Canada Red, Victoria, Cherry Red, Riverside Giant, to name a few) and is best known for its sour, eye-squeezing shut tartness that can be almost-miraculously redeemed with lots of sugar and other additives, especially strawberries. Some people abhor the taste, others acquire it, a lucky few delight in it. The key seems to be approaching it with outside-the-raised-garden-box thinking and creativity.

There's plenty of that in Lanesboro. Plenty of rhubarb, too. It grows wild here, pretty much, and is remarkably resilient. A few years ago when putting an addition on our home a wheelbarrow of wet concrete wash accidentally submerged our small rhubarb patch. I hosed it all down but some concrete did harden. End of that rhubarb, we figured. Nope. The next spring, breaking through the thawing ground and traces of cement, first in the garden as always, were little green rhubarb shoots.

Lanesboro has an average annual snowfall of 42 inches.

I once asked Mary Bell, our local rhubarb expert, what I needed to successfully grow rhubarb. "Dirt," she said. "Water. A little horse manure." Persevering and low-maintenance. My kind of plant.

Rhubarb has been around for thousands of years. The Chinese used it long ago, often as a laxative. Ben Franklin helped bring it to America. The plant looks like something in Dr. Seuss' garden, but there are dozens, probably hundreds, of tasty things you can make with it—jams, jellies, pies, muffins, relishes, syrups, salsa, juice, chili sauce, even rhubarb popcorn. Many local cooks harvest, chop and freeze it so their families can enjoy its summery taste in the middle of icy Minnesota winters. Rhubarb freezes well. So do most Minnesotans.

(Speaking of rhubarb juice...my Gramma made a batch every year in her farm kitchen. The fact that none of us kids were allowed to have any makes me think that more than juice was going on.)

People get serious about rhubarb in Lanesboro. Our neighbor called us one spring morning to politely but firmly inform us that our patch needed attention. ("You must remove those seed pods," we were told). Frank Wright's large garden just outside of town—Oz, he calls it—was a very serious rhubarb enterprise. Frank harvested nearly 1,500 pounds of it some years and sold large quantities to the local Scenic Valley Winery for their rhubarb wine.

Around 2000, a group of growers and volunteers organized a Lanesboro Farmers Market and four seasons later planned a one-day festival to promote it. That first "Rhubarb Festival" was so popular they brought it back the next year. It's now in its 13th year, planted deep and secure like the plant it celebrates.

The Festival draws big crowds, as many as 600 people. Most are local but some travel here from all over Minnesota, Iowa, Wisconsin, and points beyond. (One year, and I'm not making this up, I met a station-wagon full of nuns who'd driven here from North Dakota.) The fun starts early with Rhubarb Races that benefit the library. (Almost 200 runners showed up last year, some wearing pink-and-green tutus and P.E.T.R. shirts: "People for the Ethical Treatment of Rhubarb.") People stroll through Sylvan Park, filled with rhubarb-related food and craft booths, a petting zoo, a rhubarb fashion show (utilizing those big green leaves), and men-only pie-making contests.

And eating. Eating is a huge part of the Rhubarb Festival. You'll find hot dogs with rhubarb-ketchup, rhubarb cheesecake, strawberry-rhubarb pie, of course, rhubarb bars, cookies, and slushies. Rhu-Berry Soda Pop, too, made in nearby Spring Grove.

The main event is a tasting contest featuring dozens of rhubarb-based recipes from local cooks. Long lines of volunteer tasters wind into the Gazebo where they're handed samples of items like ginger rhubarb cordials, rhu-jerky, rhubarb-chocolate ice cream, rhubarb lace, and rhubarb-charged turkey stuffing. The entries are eaten and judged, and results are tabulated. At day's end one recipe is crowned Festival winner. This year that was Rhubarb Chile Cubano.

Nancy Martinson is a retired Lanesboro innkeeper and "Head Stalk" of the Divine Rhubarb Committee, the all-volunteer group that organizes the Festival. (The "Committee" also produced a popular rhubarb cookbook). Why is the Festival so popular, I ask? "Our tasting contest gets bigger every year," she says. "That's a big draw.

"It's also family-friendly and free," Nancy adds. 'We've had lots of good publicity, too. We've been mentioned in National Geographic, the Smithsonian, Country Living, and we're on TV almost every year. We even heard from Martha Stewart's people."

One bit of attention wasn't so positive, at least initially, she says. "We have games like the Stalk Toss to see how far you can throw one, Rhubarb Mini-Golf using stalks as clubs, and a race where you carry an egg on a stalk. We called all that the 'Rhubarb Olympics.' Then we got a cease-and-desist order from the International Olympic Committee saying we couldn't use that name. We thought it was a prank. It wasn't. We changed it to Rhu-Lympics and everybody's happy."

The Festival also provides live and lively music, kicked off by the Rhubarb Sisters leading the crowd in the Rhubarb National Anthem ("O beautiful for rhubarb stalk, for red and green and pink...for lovely green, expansive leaves, above the kitchen sink"). Today they're followed by Sweet Rhubarb, a three-lady folk group from St. Paul.

Tonight's Rhubarb Sisters concert is entitled "Awe & Rhubarb: Special Sisters Unit," promises "poetry, songs and general merriment." It doesn't disappoint. The Sisters perform a bushel-full of numbers (the majority are song parodies crafted by Sister Beth Hennessy, including "Everything's Coming Up Rhubarb" and "Rhubarb Fever"). There are other musical acts, too, like The Burdock Brothers, garden-flavored poems, and a rousing medley of "Taking a Chance on Love/The Lullaby of Rhubarb" to close the show. It all feels fun and warm and makes you wish you had room for one more piece of pie.

The Lanesboro Golf Course—the first golf course in Fillmore County—opened in 1927, and was designed by Scotland's Willie Kid, head professional at the Inter-lachen Country Club of Minneapolis in the 1920s.

Funny, yes, tasty, usually, welcome, always. Rhubarb does have a way of taking people home to long-ago backyards. "So many people have memories associated with rhubarb," says former Rhubarb Sister Robin Edmiston. "It seems strange. At the same time, it's also comforting. Rhubarb means happiness and happiness means home."

Cows in Sylvan Park, 1930s

Autumn Johnson became Lanesboro's first woman mayor in 2016.

A Visit with a Lanesboro Farmer

"I enjoy being a farmer. I was born for this kind of work."

Ed Taylor

Ed Taylor's family tree is filled with farmers. His dad was a farmer. So was his grandfather. "In the 1930s my grandfather was farming in Harmony," he says. "One day he visited Lanesboro and found some land he liked. He told my grandmother, 'If I was ten years younger I'd buy this place and work it.' 'Well, you aren't,' she said. 'Do it anyway.' He did and ended up farming there for years. Members of our family still farm it."

Ed, now in his 70s, had other dreams as a young man. After graduating from Lanesboro High in 1961 he went to college, spent a year in seminary, then traveled to Sri Lanka with the Peace Corps. He came home to work for Hormel in Austin being groomed as an office manager. "I worked in a big room with 300 desks," he remembers. "It was fine for a while. Then I knew I had to get back to the land."

Ed's boyhood memories of rural life help fuel that decision. He remembers the hard work and the grind of daily chores. But he remembers the good times, too. His eyes brighten when he talks about long-ago Saturday nights in Lanesboro when the place was alive and buzzing, filled with farm families come-to-town for their weekly shopping, people visiting neighbors in the aisles of the hardware store, kids seeing movies at the Elite Theater, families eating ice cream at the White Front Café.

When Ed left Hormel he came back to farm with his father. He and his wife, Verna, raised a family on their Lanesboro farm. "It was a good life," he says. "Not always easy, though. We struggled for years. Never had a lot of money. Verna handled the paperwork. I did the physical labor. It all seemed to work."

Farmers like Ed faced challenges farming here, the same challenges faced by the first farmers of Fillmore County. Many immigrants in the 19th century had been farmers in the "old country." They arrived with hopes of farming again. When President Abraham Lincoln signed the Homestead Act of 1862 offering free 160-acre parcels to citizens willing to stay on the property for five years and improve it, they were eager to sign on. They worked hard to overcome the driftless geography of rolling hills and steep valleys and concentrated on wheat that could be ground into flour at the

The local wheat harvest of the early 1870s was estimated at 20-30 bushels an acre.

local mills. A local outbreak of "wheat smut" in the late 1870s damaged crops and slowed the area's entire economy. Some farmers left, new crops were tried, and livestock became more prevalent. But farming has been and remains a bedrock industry of southeast Minnesota.

"Nutrient-wise, the land around here is really good," Ed explains, "but the soil is highly erodible. You need to farm it carefully. Lots of soil was lost. It's still being lost. Look at the Lanesboro Dam after a heavy rain and you'll see lots of brown, muddy water washing over it. That always bothers me."

Farming in the late 1800s

Today Ed has a 300-acre dairy farm just south of Lanesboro that he bought in 1982. He has around 450 cows and milks 200. He's seen many changes over the years. "Farmers here have moved away from livestock," he says. "They're doing more plowing and growing lots more corn. Used to be oats, barley, and alfalfa here, even tobacco in the '40s and '50s, especially near Whalan. Not much corn back then. Now it dominates."

Farming has changed. So have farmers. "Years back not many farmers had formal education," Ed says. "When I came back after getting a degree, some people asked why I'd done that. Today most farmers are college-trained. Better farm management is stressed. That certainly helps."

When Ed's family put down roots here, farms were smaller and family-run. Today only 1 in 4 operate like that. Farms are bigger and often rented out. The classic old farmhouses we see on local country roads most often have non-farming families living in them. More than a few sit empty.

Lots of reasons explain the changes, says Ed. Small farms are less viable now and often get purchased by bigger farms. Families are smaller, and when kids go away to college it's less likely they'll return to help run the family farm. Farmers, like everyone, get older and retire. Roller-coaster farm economies present yearly challenges. So do new technologies and buzzwords like GMOs and organic crops.

Ed hung tight to that roller-coaster. He vividly remembers the farm crisis of the '70s that hit Lanesboro like everywhere else. "Young tigers bought too much land and had too much debt," Ed recalls. "Some ended up losing their farms. All of us were nervous. It was tough on the town, too. You could fire a cannon down Main Street and not hit anything except a few cars in front of a liquor store. The future didn't look so good for Lanesboro."

Ed was a farmer. He also cared about his town. Along with a half-dozen other young couples, he and Verna helped organize what they called the "Community Club" to brainstorm how to help Lanesboro survive. He served on the School Board and volunteered where he could. "It was all part of trying to help," he says.

Farming changes, life changes. Verna passed in 2015. Today Ed looks to the future through the eyes of his kids and grandkids. He's optimistic, he says. "Farming is better now. You don't hear of too many people selling. We had 4-5 years of excellent corn prices. Those have dropped some, so have milk prices. It just means people have to work harder and smarter."

Hard work on a farm has been Ed Taylor's life. He wouldn't have it any other way. "It's been a good life," he says. "I'm so thankful that Verna and I could raise our kids in a rural life. It's exactly what we wanted to do."

Tobacco farming was an early bluff country crop that led to the production of locally-made cigars called "The Pride of Lanesboro."

A Play at the Commonweal Theatre

"The minute you walk in the door at the Commonweal,
you feel like you're a part of something special."

PJ Thompson, Commonweal MDC Member

You'll find some of Lanesboro's simplest and most enduring pleasures (mixed with a healthy portion of imagination) on the north end of Parkway Avenue in a building that used to be a cheese factory. You wouldn't know that today. What's there now is the Commonweal Theatre Company presenting an award-winning, consistently high-level of acting and production that's been delighting the people of Lanesboro and the entire region for almost thirty years.

How did all this happen? In 1989 the Lanesboro Arts Council had one of those "let's try something and see how it works" kind-of-ideas that this town is so good at. Their idea was to offer a summer theater season in the then-dark St. Mane Theater. The Council approached local theater student Eric Bunge to see if he'd be interested in pulling it together. Eric ran it by some friends. "Sure, let's do it," they said. Plays were selected, auditions held, sets built, and rehearsals were planned. They'd give it a one-season try.

It worked. Did it ever. By summer's end nearly 3,000 people had enjoyed an 11-week, 40-performance season of "A Midsummer Night's Dream" and "Crimes of the Heart." The plays, featuring ten local actors, worked with a budget of just over $20,000. It went so well that plans were made to try it again the next summer.

The Commonweal has been "trying that again" so successfully that they've developed into a rarity: a financially successful, locally-based professional theater company with full-time, resident actors. All of that in a town of less than 800 people.

The Commonweal's current season runs April through December with five plays that include dramas, comedies, musicals and contemporary works. Their 180-200 performances a year bring in a yearly audience of more than 21,000 people. Its core-base of full-time actors hold down a variety of different roles in the Theater.

The Commonweal Theatre presented 20 years of Henrik Ibsen Festivals (the last one in 2017) that commissioned eight new adaptations of Ibsen plays from playwright Jeffrey Hatcher.

The Commonweal Theater

"The great thing about the Commonweal is the deep connection we have with our audience," says Hal Cropp who joined the company in 1992 and has served as either Artistic or Executive Director for nearly 25 years. "Because of our artist-administrator model, people will not only see me on stage on Friday night, but Saturday afternoon they may walk into the box-office and I'm there selling them their tickets, or on Saturday night I'm the guy behind the counter pouring their wine."

Over the years the Commonweal has also created an apprentice program, offered traveling productions in schools around the state, hosted Elderhostel programs, and created an internationally-acclaimed Ibsen Festival. The budget for this nonprofit has grown to $750,000, supported by ticket sales, grant support, and hundreds of happy donors from Lanesboro, southern Minnesota, northern Iowa and western Wisconsin. One estimate is that it adds approximately $3-million dollars annually into the economy of southeast Minnesota.

The story of the Commonweal Theatre—"drama unfolds where the Root River bends"—goes beyond numbers. This is a Lanesboro "place" that takes you places.

You might float "Around the World in 80 Days." You might sleuth with Sherlock Holmes' through foggy Victorian London. You might saunter the dusty trails of 1930s Oklahoma with Woody Guthrie. You might hear lilting Irish brogues "Outside Mullingar." You might navigate the always-modern social and political complexities of Henrik Ibsen's 19th century Norway. Come in, take a seat, get ready to travel, in mind and spirit.

Tonight I'm at the Commonweal to see a production of "Souvenir," a play by Stephen Temperley that first came to Broadway in 2005. It tells the true story of Florence Foster Jenkins, a music-loving, supremely confident but musically-challenged coloratura soprano who made a brief but memorable splash in New York in the 1940s. Commonweal casts are usually small and you might see multiple roles played by a single actor in the same play. Tonight's two-person play fits that style perfectly. They do a lot with a little at the Commonweal Theatre.

This is a Monday night in late August and the theater—capacity 200—is comfortably filled with a mix of local residents and tourists. Many tourists come to town to bike. Many also come primarily to attend plays at the Commonweal. You'll meet many people who see every play every season, and many who attend a single play multiple times. "You see new things, think about new things, and learn new things at every performance," says one long-time patron.

The audience enjoys those plays in a beautiful little theater with a thrust stage surrounded by seats on three sides. That stage and those seats (none of which are more than 35 feet from the stage) were both rescued from the original Guthrie Theater in Minneapolis. It's all showcased in a space beautifully renovated in 2007 in a $3.5 million dollar capital campaign. From the storefronts on the theater's façade to the fascinating artwork of local artist Karl Unnasch called the "Commonweal Stash", the entire place is a work of art. Look up at the ceiling—you'll see flying shovel, pitchforks, Canada geese and more. (Don't miss the restrooms!) Tours of the theater are available.

Tonight's story is a good one, funny but thoughtful, too, with insights about the nature of music, art, life itself really (what's the difference between the way we see ourselves and the way the world sees us—and does it really matter?). It's a fun story with believable characters, and pleasant jazz piano interludes move everything along, interspersed with Miss Jenkins' almost-scary wailings. The ending is sweet-sad and brings the audience to its feet with a fully-deserved (not just Minnesota-nice) standing ovation for actors Stela Burdt and Stephen Houtz. The performance closes with a friendly invitation for audience members to visit with the actors in Commonweal's "Encore" reception hall next door.

A movie about Jenkins starring Meryl Streep is in national release the same week I see the play. The Commonweal needn't worry about comparison. "Meryl needs to come watch Stela play this part," the lady next to me says with total sincerity. "She'd learn a few things!" I agree.

People love the Commonweal and are loyal to it. The Million Dollar Club invites donors to pledge a minimum annual supporting gift to help sustain and expand the work of the theater. They're all supporting a nonprofit, artistic endeavor of which they—and Lanesboro itself—can be very proud. In the fall of 2017 the Company received a Minnesota Nonprofit Award for Excellence from the Minnesota Council of Nonprofits, one of just six given in the entire state, and the first of these awards to be bestowed on a professional theater company.

"Underpinning (everything we do)," explained Cropp in remarks he made when accepting that award, "is a company culture that embraces the concept that anyone who walks through our doors is made to feel that the Commonweal is their theater, their home."

That's exactly how it feels. A warm, welcoming, soul-expanding home. One you want to visit often. So many people, from this little town of Lanesboro and beyond, are eagerly doing just that.

Commonweal Theatre's 2007 capital campaign donors are honored by 250 small mason jars in the theater lobby that contain personalized "symbols," such as a scrabble tile, a golf ball, a sea shell, and a miniature cow.

A Night in a Lanesboro B & B

Every time we open our door, it's like reading the pages of a new book.

A visit to Lanesboro means making big decisions. What will you do today? Bike, shop, tube the river, take an Amish tour, enjoy a fun restaurant, see a play, listen to live music? So many choices, so little time. That's part of the fun.

If you plan to be here overnight, another choice confronts you. Where will you sleep? Maybe you're tent-camping or have an RV, but if you need a room you're in luck. Lanesboro is the official "Bed & Breakfast Capital of Minnesota," and has more than a dozen local B & Bs eager to offer you a comfortable bed and fine breakfast. If you've never been to one, or if you're a B &B veteran, it's a great choice. It might end up the highlight of your trip.

I'm not partial on this, of course. Susie and I have owned and operated Anna V's Bed & Breakfast in Lanesboro since 2009. It's been an amazing experience. Doing it in Lanesboro makes it all the better. We're part of a business enterprise that goes back centuries. (Think Bethlehem).The long-established European B & B concept arrived in colonial America when roads were rough and trips were long. Later, before

Anna V's Bed and Breakfast

motels came on the scene, travelers looked to inns or private homes for safe places and warm meals. In the Great Depression $2 a night was a common price for an overnight stay. In the 1950s many Americans visited Europe, stayed in B & Bs, and returned home with good memories. Soon B & Bs were popping up across this country.

There are nearly 17,000 inns and B & Bs in the U.S. today. Many are in beautiful historic homes and offer full, even elegant, breakfasts. (No lunches or dinners normally). Prices have increased. So have services and amenities. State inspectors keep tabs on them, and while the web-driven, less regulated "Air B-and-B" industry is expanding, traditional B & Bs are here to stay. Many travelers, having tried them once, never return to more traditional lodging.

Why are there so many B & Bs in Lanesboro? The town's resurgence in the mid-1980s, ignited by the new bike trail and expanding art scene, brought an influx of tourists needing overnight lodging. Soon stately Victorian homes built by long-ago Lanesboro families like the Scanlans, Habberstads, and Thompsons opened their doors to fill that lodging need. B & Bs in Lanesboro were a perfect fit and continue to flourish today.

One particular Lanesboro B & B didn't just benefit from the town's renewed energy—it helped start it. In the 1980's Jack and Nancy Bratrud of Minneapolis purchased an historic downtown stone building, for many years the Thompson Brothers Furniture Store, and transformed it into Mrs. B's Historic Inn. Their luxury rooms, five-course dining (some people still rave about it), and friendly hospitality attracted local and national media attention. Not to mention lots of customers. Before long, Mrs. B's success jump-started other downtown business ventures and added to Lanesboro's new momentum.

How does staying at a bed-and-breakfast compare to a Hilton, Hyatt or Holiday Inn? Today's B & Bs (unlike a generation ago) offer private bathrooms, air conditioning, Wi-Fi and more. The main difference is location—a B & B puts you in a town, often in a home in a neighborhood of that town, and gives your stay a personal touch hard to match.

Food is a big deal at B & Bs. Most innkeepers take pride in creating breakfasts you'll remember, such as Mexican egg bake, wild rice-and-ham quiche, pepper bacon, blueberry-maple sausages, white chocolate & raspberry scones. Lanesboro's rural roots make farm-to-table a natural here. Fresh-from-the-garden asparagus to heirloom tomatoes to Yukon Gold potatoes (we get ours from Doris at the Farmer's Market) are local highlights. One morning we truthfully told our guests that we knew the name of the chicken who laid the eggs for their omelets. That's local and fresh.

B & Bs are about people most of all. Guests meet other guests. (As much as they'd like, that is—some visit, others prefer quiet, whatever works). Conversation around a common table can be fun and a stimulating way to connect with people. Interests are shared, connections are made, and strangers can become friends. A rare treat in our screen-saturated world.

Our doorbell rings and it feels like we're opening the pages of a new book. We don't know who we'll meet or what we'll learn. People come here from all over: Minnesota, Iowa, Wisconsin, Chicagoland, mostly, but also from across the country, even around the world. Our breakfasts this year have welcomed guests from Norway, Colombia, New York, Japan, and the U. K. They might also live in Rollingstone, Minnesota. You just never know.

Who are these people? We've met teachers, doctors, artists, nurses, plumbers, accountants and farmers. We've also hosted a former Minnesota governor, athletes (a number of world-class bikers), a Pulitzer Prize-winning cartoonist, writers, and musicians. One Sunday morning a space-scientist enthralled us with the details of his job of helping to steer the Mars rovers. The sculptor who created Goldy Gopher on the U of M campus (and Sid Hartman's Target Center statue) was here recently, so was a weatherman who works in Antarctica. We also meet extraordinary "ordinary" people—anniversary folks, honeymooners, students, grandparents, you name it. Their stories, humor and inspiration are gifts that make each stay unique.

We make friends. We laugh. I'm writing this in early April. This morning a sweet, quiet lady from Wisconsin came down for breakfast looking unnerved, frightened even. "There's a problem upstairs," she told me, near tears. "There's a huge spider in our shower!" I grabbed a broom and raced upstairs, when I heard her call out behind me: "One more thing—April Fools!" She got me.

A relaxed breakfast table with a third cup of coffee. A cozy parlor with a fireplace on a snowy day. A porch swing on a summer evening watching the flicker of fireflies. Those are the moments that make a B & B stay something people don't forget. Combine all that with the simple pleasures of this little town and you've got something special. Think about giving a Lanesboro B & B a try. We can leave the light on for you, too.

Lanesboro has more licensed B & B's than any other town in Minnesota.

A Winter Day in Lanesboro

So quiet you can hear a snowflake land.

There's a question we hear frequently at our B &B breakfast table that always surprises us. On a bright, sunny, summer morning someone will ask: "What's Lanesboro like in the winter?" I always give the same answer. "Quiet," I say. "Very quiet. But beautiful, too. Almost like an entirely different place."

If warm-weather Lanesboro seems hidden, then winter totally buries this place. Blessed are those who find it. Winter makes it harder to get here and slower to move around in once you arrive. But totally worth it. In a recent listicle entitled "10 Enchanting Minnesota Towns That Feel Like You've Fallen Into A Snow Globe," Lanesboro came in #3 (behind Stillwater and New Ulm). That captures the winter beauty of this village very well.

I'm writing this on a wintry January morning while looking out the third-floor window-nook of our Brooklyn neighborhood home. A large weather system stretching from Wyoming to western Wisconsin just dumped 6" of new snow here overnight. It feels more like a March storm, though. The snow is wet and heavy and is sticking to evergreen trees and houses like thick vanilla frosting. I must be hungry right now. When I look out at the light snow covering the bluffs circling Lanesboro, it also looks like a dusting of powdered sugar.

Plows were out early this morning. Streets have been cleared, salt has been spread. Schools are closed, which is rare for here. I'll need to shovel our sidewalk and porch steps later. Not my favorite thing in the world. But there's much to enjoy in a day like this, too.

Let's face reality. This is Minnesota. Winter can be harsh here. Snowstorms clog streets. Driving can be hazardous. (Especially on the steep grades of County Road 8 or on Church Hill). So can walking. Just ask our neighbor, Nancy, who went out to walk her dog last week, a pretty ordinary thing to do, hit an ice patch, and returned home with a broken wrist. Piercing wind chills that can hit 30 and 40 below bring on ice-cream headaches. Winters here can be draining and drag on far too long. Some Lanesboro snow-birds we know are enjoying breakfast this morning next to a

"The Norski Winter Fest" was an early winter-themed Lanesboro event that eventually led to the Ibsen Festival at the Commonweal.

sparkling pool in Florida. No shoveling for them today. Lucky people. But they're missing something, too. Something very special.

What is Lanesboro like in the winter? So quiet you swear you can hear snowflakes land. Downtown shops and restaurants reduce hours. Many are already closed for the season. The Commonweal Theatre stage lies dark until mid-April. There aren't as many reasons to be in Lanesboro in the winter as in other seasons. If you do make your way here, you'll have the place pretty much to yourself. That's not necessarily a bad thing. A snowy winter day + a fireplace + a good book = a pretty great day, don't you think?

From time to time discussions flare up in our lodging and tourist promotion groups about making Lanesboro a 12-month destination point. It would make economic sense to get visitors here year around. Feels like we're swimming a bit upstream, though. Efforts to accomplish that have had limited success to this point. "I'm not sure I like the year-round idea," one downtown merchant honestly told me. "After all the rush I enjoy the quiet season. It gives time to take a breath and re-charge."

The winter weather slows everything down. Homes and businesses button up. You can get outside. Bundle up, be brave (and careful), go for a walk on a crisp, star-filled night. It can feel other-worldly. If it's below-zero cold the snow crunches under each step. In the distance you might hear the muffled scrapping of someone clearing a driveway or chopping patches of stubborn ice. Winter often seems to be winning, but that's fine. Surrender and enjoy.

Lanesboro residents make the most of winter. Locals find morning coffee and news at the Pastry Shop or the Cracked Egg. Cross-country skiers hit the trail. Lanesboro School elementary kids still get outside at recess, sliding down Sylvan Park hills in scenes from a Grandma Moses painting. Snow sculpture contests, candlelight skis, and St. Mane concerts create popular gathering places. "Turkey bowling" took over Parkway Avenue on February night a few winters ago. Chili feeds and potlucks warm people up. Commuters work from home if possible. Winter life goes on, and people enjoy the quiet in their own ways.

Winter slows and shooshes people in Lanesboro, another gift in a noisy world. Sure, we're glad when green stalks of rhubarb push up through the snow and the "Opening April 1st" sign appears in the window of the "Another Time" ice cream shop. But let's not rush it.

Just now outside my window a crimson-red cardinal landed on our bird feeder. Top that, summer biker friends. I love the warm weather, too. I look forward to having you all back, along with the fun on Lanesboro streets and trails. But when that all happens, a part of me will actually miss the comforting isolation that winter creates here.

Time to get back to shoveling? Yes, I'll bundle up and do it. All pleasures have a price. But...it can wait. Time for one more marshmallow in the hot chocolate. What's winter like in Lanesboro? Quiet, very quiet. Almost like an entirely different place.

Gazebo in Sylvan Park

Ice was harvested each winter in large "cakes" from Mill Pond and stored in sawdust for use in spring and summer.

Lanesboro... Its People

Dr. Drake and friend, 1913

"I came, I saw, and I was conquered...the village of Lanesboro seemed...desirable because of the beauty of its surroundings, the longevity, intelligence and culture of its inhabitants, and its claim as a business point...with a future (to be) developed by the energy of its...businessmen." (George Harding, 1880, why he moved here from Indianapolis)

Lanesboro...Its People

We've explored Lanesboro's colorful past. We've visited places that make it unique. Let's move to what leaves the deepest impression of this town: the people. The ones who live here, the ones who visit, the weekenders, the tourists. The ones in town, the ones from the country. All the people of Lanesboro.

One of the first things to say about them is that they're friendly. I've heard many others say the same thing, both long-time residents and visitors. People here are nice and it's more than just casual "Minnesota nice." People here are genuine. They're authentic. They have a refreshing openness about them.

"In Lanesboro we error on the side of assuming that people are good," a local resident told me recently. "Sure, there's quirkiness here, too, and moments of cynicism. But those don't dominate. People like being here and they like the other people who are here." Another friend says "Lanesboro is the least judgmental place I've ever experienced."

What does local friendliness look like? When you walk into a Lanesboro store, a bank, or a restaurant, you meet people who are genuinely happy to see and serve you. They know your name or will ask it. When people ask how you are, they actually listen to your answer. You feel prompted to do the same.

A long-time resident has a theory about why this is true. "Everyone in Lanesboro is here because they made a choice to be here," she says. "They weren't transferred here for their job. Nothing forced them to be here. They're here because they want to be here. That makes a big difference."

I agree. When you visit or live here, you find yourself mixing with good people who enjoy their town, the quality of life it offers, and the people who create its community. That makes it better...for everyone.

Let's meet the people of Lanesboro.

In 1902, Mr. Charlie Lee, originally from Canton, China, opened a Chinese laundry in the basement of what is now the Lanesboro History Museum.

Who Are They?

People here work hard, play hard, and share a special spirit.

Who are the people of Lanesboro and what are they like? What's most important to them? Where do they work? What do they do in their free time? There aren't one-size-fits all answers to those questions, of course. But they're fun to think about if you're trying to capture the essence of this unique town.

Generally speaking people in Lanesboro are down-home and down-to-earth. You might expect that in the Midwest, and that's part of it. But it goes deeper. People here genuinely care about other people. Family and friends are a major part of their lives. People are valued here. They're a priority.

People here work hard, too. Many still farm. Most commute daily to full-time jobs. They find those mostly in Rochester, about 45 minutes away, where the Mayo Clinic is a big employer. (Mayo sends a daily bus down this way to help make that work). Others find jobs in cities Chatfield, Rushford, Winona or across the river in La Crosse, Wisconsin. The work ethic here is strong. Take a drive outside of town on a late fall evening and you'll see farmers still working in their fields, harvesting crops by headlights.

Locally the Lanesboro school and day care center provide important jobs. So does the tourist "industry" with its restaurants, coffee shops, lodging, gift stores, bike and river outfitters, Amish tours, and more. The arts community (theaters, galleries, individual artist studios) creates employment, too.

Yes, Lanesboro people work hard. They also play hard. Many here love to hunt and fish. Families play together and keep busy together in school activities. Moms, dads, extended family and friends cheer for the Lanesboro High School Burros under Friday night lights (they play 9-man football here) and in the school gym for basketball and volleyball games. Kids play pick-up basketball in Sylvan Park, go tubing, sliding and sledding in the winter, enjoy their proms and graduations, and just hang out like kids everywhere. Church life is important, too, from Sunday worship to baptisms, confirmation, youth groups, and choirs. Currently congregational life in town is centered at Bethlehem Lutheran Church and the Discovery Faith Community (formerly the Methodist Church), with a smaller group attending St. Patrick's Catholic Church.

People like big-time sports here, of course. Along with the Burros, Lanesboro roots for the Minnesota Gophers. (Iowa is close enough that you'll run into an occasional Hawkeye or Cardinal). The Minnesota Vikings rule (one of our Fillmore Avenue neighbors blows a loud horn every time they score a touchdown), but you'll find some Packer lovers, too. Twins caps and jerseys are popular. More than a few locals trek up to Target Field for Twins games each summer. Many make that same trek north for the Minnesota State Fair at the end of August.

People in Lanesboro enjoy food and drink, of course. Hemingway called Paris a "moveable feast." I nominate Lanesboro as a "moveable potluck." They're everywhere. Church dinners (Norwegian meatballs, chicken, lefse, even a bit of lutefisk), Legion fish fries always draw crowds. Thirsty people hear find cold beer at the High Court Pub, the Legion and the Root River Saloon, martinis at Riverside on the Root, wine at The Granary, Spring Grove Pop at Lulu's Playhouse. A few local restaurants have outside decks and great river views for warm summer days. The Cracked Egg, the Spud Boy Diner, and the Pastry Shop keep morning coffee cups filled and conversation flowing.

Politically-speaking, it's kind of a mix. Fillmore County went heavily red in 2016 but Lanesboro has a blue-ish tint. People travel often, for business and pleasure. Recent conversations caught me up on their visits from Branson to Budapest, from Tuscany to Tucson. Many escape Minnesota winters by heading south to Florida and Arizona. The majority nestles in at home year 'round, where they work hard, walk their dogs, go to book clubs, local concerts, art shows, and yoga classes, and mostly savor the priceless routines of family and friends.

Who are the people of Lanesboro? Simple answers won't cover it for everybody. Common threads do run through this place, though, shared traits, values and characteristics that create what you could call the "Lanesboro spirit." Here are five elements I see.

Orval Amdahl—a World War II Marine—returned home to Lanesboro with a souvenir: a samurai sword. In a 2013 ceremony that received international attention, Orval returned the sword to the son of the sword's original owner. "I believe in peace," said Orv.

The Spirit of Lanesboro:
People Here Love Nature

"There's no place on earth more beautiful than the bluff area of southeast Minnesota."
David J. Tacke

The people of Lanesboro love the natural beauty of this place. More than a few will say it's the one main reason they live and visit here. They treasure its forests, rivers, bluff country views, rolling hills, and panoramic horizons. People go for walks, ride bikes and motorcycles, and take drives in the country to enjoy all that. The fact that it's so accessible makes it even better. Quite a show, all for free.

On summer evenings neighbors relax on porches under star-filled skies. In fall maple trees burst with orange, yellow and red color on Parkway Avenue next to Sylvan Park. Winter brings white dustings of snow on the bluffs, clouds of steam rising off the river by the Lanesboro Dam, and thick snow clinging to evergreen trees. Spring means new life, gardens sprouting and farmers tilling and planting their fields. All four seasons bring different scenic pleasures.

Some people get up closer to nature here by heading out on the Root River in canoes, kayaks and tubes. Many fish in local streams, the finest trout streams in the state. Tourists park their tents, trailers and RVs here to camp and relax. Spots are available in two city-owned lots as well as the 250 Campground and Eagle Cliff.

Two couples from the Twin Cities, all busy, successful professionals, return to our B & B for Memorial Day weekend every year. They have an annual tradition when they arrive. On their first evening here they go for a walk on the trail just past the Dam to a meadow that is filled that time of year with "singing frogs." They sit, they listen, they soak it all in. "It's a highlight of our year," they tell me.

Nature seems to refresh, invigorate and inspire the people of Lanesboro. Maybe there's something mystical in that. Since the 1980s thousands of people in Japan have enthusiastically embraced the practice of "shinrin-yoku" or "forest bathing." On weekends they leave their homes in crowded cities to visit parks and forest areas where they walk and hike but mostly relax. They believe—and recent medical studies

In December, 2014, a wayward moose walked through a local neighborhood headed in the direction of Iowa.

apparently confirm—that forested outdoor settings exude natural stress-healing compounds. A century ago visitors were encouraged to visit southeastern Minnesota to benefit from its "healthy air." Perhaps people have been taking Lanesboro "forest baths" for a long time without even knowing it!

The people of Lanesboro love where they live and a major part of that is appreciating the area's natural beauty. Like everywhere, life can get busy. We too often neglect to take time to smell the flowers. That happens here, too. But there's so much to explore and enjoy here that you make that time. People do. It's a priceless part of the Lanesboro spirit.

"Lover's Lane"

"I'll be walking to my office downtown on an early spring morning when the sun is just reaching the top of the bluffs, and it's all so quiet and beautiful, and I'll think, 'you just can't top this.'" (Tom Manion)

The Spirit of Lanesboro:
People Here Are Active

Staying active seems routine here—in many ways, for all ages.

The people of Lanesboro love being active. Many are regular walkers, hikers, bikers, and joggers. They take yoga classes. They walk their dogs. (One of our neighbors takes his Airedale for a shared daily bike/run). People of all ages work out at the Coffee Street Fitness Center. This area has attracted many people who make physical activity and good health a priority in their lives. That's good for them. Inspiring, too.

Staying active is about exercise and good health. It's also about having fun. Three years ago Lanesboro was designated an "American Play City" by Kaboom, a national non-profit that helps communities build playgrounds. That label fits this town well. People play here. We saw that on our first visit. People were riding bikes, canoeing and tubing on the river, and hiking on the trail. We saw people carrying fishing poles, heading up to the Lanesboro Golf Course, and playing Frisbee in the park. Lots of active people playing and enjoying life.

Some people here take staying active very seriously. Jeff Kamm worked for nearly thirty years at Mayo as a mental health counsellor. In the 1970s, like many people then, a daily run became part of Jeff's exercise routine. Unlike many, he never stopped. Now approaching 70, this Vietnam vet has competed in 324 races, including marathons, half-marathons, 10Ks and 5Ks. The shelves in his Lanesboro home display 110 medals and trophies, 80 for finishing first, second or third in his age group. "Running is a part of my life year-round," says Jeff. "It's like breathing for me." He has no intention of slowing down. "500 races seems a great goal," he says. "No reason to stop now."

Being active and playing is more than sports and exercise. People in Lanesboro play in many ways and they do that year around. They attend local theater, go to music concerts, enjoy family reunions and picnics in Sylvan Park, go camping, shop in downtown stores, browse art galleries. Minnesota winters can be snowy and cold,

"Lanesboro is an amazing community. For a town so small it feels so big because there's so much going on." (Bailey Cahlander, Minneapolis artist)

but people here cross-country ski and snow-shoe. Kids grab their sleds and head for the hill by the school. After the season's first big snowfall, the first sound you'll hear is the revving of snowmobile engines.

Some of our Lanesboro friends mix exercise and adventure. Six of them spent a month last fall biking the Danube Trail that passes through Germany, Austria and Hungary. We met a local man who raised bees and sold honey to fund his climb of Mt. Kilimanjaro. Two other Lanesboro friends got back recently from running a marathon in Vancouver. Lanesboro's active and playful spirit travels well!

It ages well, too. We've met great role models here, men and women in their 60's, 70's and 80's, who stay active, play hard, and have fun. Our farmer friend Ed Taylor is a common sight racing around town on his bicycle as is Carlos from the Cottage Street Inn who bikes bluff country—and around the world. Mary, a former Lanesboro innkeeper, now 70, drives to remote Mexican villages each Easter to deliver cupcakes, hugs and love to kids in need. Our B & B guest Ellen added an item to her bucket list on her 50th birthday: over the next decade she plans to bike in all 50 states. Jeanne, nearing 80, still tees it up three times a week at her local golf course. Stan, in his early 70s, showed me a draft of a play he'd recently finished. "My first," he told me, with a proud smile.

Staying active, through work, play, hobbies, or volunteer service, is definitely woven into the Lanesboro spirit. It makes all kinds of sense, for many different reasons, no matter where you call home. It doesn't have an expiration date, either. Grab your shoes again, let's make that happen.

The Spirit of Lanesboro:
People Here Are Creative

"Creativity is interconnected here. The valleys and bluffs invite artistic expression. So does our good blend of creative souls."

Joan Finnegan

The spirit of Lanesboro has a creative streak. That's very obvious in the beautiful work of local artists, painters, photographers, jewelry makers, and crafters. Visit the Lanesboro Arts Gallery, the Black Crow on Coffee Street (or Man Art next door), go on local Art Crawls, stop in at stores like Windy Mesa (where David Applen has been making and selling jewelry here for 26 years), or Crown Trout Jewelers where Liz Bucheit does her nationally-acclaimed goldsmith wizardry, and you'll be amazed at the quality and world-class craftsmanship of Lanesboro artists.

Lanesboro creativity goes beyond "typical" art, though. Creativity happens here, too, when people have new ideas, try new things, and take some risks. It might be someone deciding to learn how to paint. It might be starting a new business. It might be acting in a play. It might be strumming a guitar or finally writing a story that's been in your head for years. Maybe it's coming up with new rhubarb recipe. Creativity takes people all kinds of places in Lanesboro.

That's been true for a long time. The town founders arrived here 150 years ago with creative—some might say risky—ideas: let's build a town! let's put in a dam! let's create a lake! They pulled all of that off in less than two years. Amazing.

Creative souls have followed their heart for years here. Rudy Elstad grew up in the Brooklyn neighborhood of Lanesboro in the 1920s. After technical training and work in a Minneapolis ad agency, in 1938 he became an animator for Walt Disney and contributed animation to classic films like "Fantasia" (he drew the Nutcracker Suite fairies and worked for a six weeks on the "Sun-God" chariot scene that appeared in the film for four seconds!) and "Bambi" (where he created Bambi's mother).

Inspiration can live in one person. It can also be contagious. A person gets an idea. They tell it to someone else. The idea grows, gets tweaked, momentum builds,

"You find interesting and dynamic people here. Lanesboro seems to be a hub for deep-thinking people." (Renee Bergstrom)

the fun begins. That happens around here–that 1930's Mickey Rooney/Andy Hardy movie spirit, "hey, kids, let's put on a show!"

Look at what that "contagious inspiration" has created in Lanesboro over the years. Art in the Park. The Commonweal Theatre. The Rhubarb Festival. The Rhubarb Sisters (who begat the Rutabaga Brothers who begat Turnip Truck). Over The Back Fence. The Annual Holiday Sing-a-Long. Silent Movies in the Park. History Alive! Pop-Up-Plays. Others events and activities, too. Sure, some things get tried that don't last. (Drag shows at the Sons of Norway come to mind.) You move on, try something else. That's fine. Be creative. Take new risks. Most of all, have fun!

Artist-actor Bebe Keith says it's the people of this place, and their can-do spirit, that builds artistic momentum. "Lanesboro has so many creative people to draw upon," Bebe says. "When I thought it would be fun to make silent movies, I knew it would be possible. I knew I'd find plenty of people willing to be part of the project. I knew I'd be able to get permission to use the park and to save a building as a backup location in case of rain. I knew I'd find an audience who would come to see the movies. That doesn't happen just anywhere. Lanesboro has a special magic. If you're willing to take the bull by the horns and try something new, you'll likely succeed here!"

People also end up trying creative things they've wanted to try for years but never had the opportunity (or courage) to attempt. Until now. Until here. In Lanesboro they go for it. They act, sing, write poems, bake pies, start a clothing shop, refurbish a house, try kayaking, jump into local politics, try (even teach) yoga. Our friends Robert and Cindy have created an amazing day lily farm just outside of town where Robert hand-pollinates plants to create hundreds of gorgeous, multi-hued varieties. I think of Arv Fabian who turned an auto parts store into Das Wurst Haus, the liveliest little restaurant you'd could ever hope to find, with Arv on his concertina, his wife on the piano, home-made root beer (and mustard), and a joyful friendliness that people still talk about (and miss) years after he retired. Lanesboro Community Theater and History Alive! Lanesboro have been the grateful recipients of costumes designed by Linda Watson—all hand-sewn, all exquisite. "I love doing it," says this grandmother of four who flunked home economics but now designs and creates costumes for casts as

"Lanesboro gives people a place and the freedom to pursue their dreams." (Caleb Lauritsen)

large as 60 members. "People have enough realism in their lives these days," she said in a recent news interview. "They want to see some fantasy." Linda creates just that, in living color. That's creativity.

That list can go on. "People gain confidence here," says Sandy Webb, a retired teacher who moved to Lanesboro in 2010 and now sings at "Over the Back Fence" and acts in community theater. "They see that it's okay to take risks so they go for it. People blossom in Lanesboro!"

My neighbor, Bill, is a retired painter. Bebe knew Bill had some piano background, and a few years ago she asked him if he'd ever played the accordion. No, Bill said. "Want to learn?" Bill's response was pure Lanesboro. "Why not?" A little practice and a few months later, Bill, Bebe, Lynn Susag, and Rocky Haddorf created "Accordionation," a squeezebox ensemble that played at the Rhubarb Festival and "wherever people would listen," they say. Bill even played a solo accordion number in a recent community theater production.

"I never saw myself being on stage," Bill says. "That was way beyond my comfort zone. Now you have to drag me off. You're up there and you feel the audience pulling for you. They want you to succeed."

Creative risk-taking takes many forms. Blake and Caleb moved to Lanesboro a few years ago to escape what they call urban "cube life," bought a hobby farm, started a "barn sales antique" business, and now run the town's corner grocery store. Oh yes, they also have a thriving (world-wide) internet-Lego business (PlanetBrick.com) that they run from the 2nd floor of the grocery store. Those kind of people get inspired in Lanesboro. They also inspire others.

If we had time I could tell you one more story. The one about a one-time Baptist pastor who now bakes scones in a Lanesboro B &B and who did a little singing-and-dancing in a Lanesboro musical last summer. Who knows? Maybe there's a story like that in your future, too.

"There's a mystery to Lanesboro. The big sky, the trail by the river, space to think, dream and create. It hooks people." (Carla Noack)

The Spirit of Lanesboro:
People Here Build Community

"Lanesboro people are social."

Lanesboro Leader, early 1900s

Community is big in Lanesboro. People here like to connect with other people. Apparently they always have. It's a place where people know your name, or if they don't, they'd like to find out. You find out their name, too. When you see someone walking their dog, it's a good bet you know the dog's name.

Community happens naturally with family and friends, of course, but other places, too. Small groups form, book clubs, church circles, Bible studies, poker games. You aren't close friends with everybody, of course, but in Lanesboro people matter. Community is important. That's where people talk, listen, learn, create, laugh, make friends, find support and enjoy friendship. Community makes life better, for everybody. People here realize that and make it a priority.

Maybe that's more important in a town whose population is south of 1,000. Small towns foster interdependence. We know we need everybody. You all stick together to make sure it keeps working. You know that it helps to buy groceries at the Parkway Market, pizza at The Bite, or gas at the local BP. Prices might be a bit higher (not always). But it's helping your neighbors. People think about that here.

"Lanesboro has layers of really good people," says Linda Tacke, who moved here ten years ago with her husband, David, from Minnetonka, Minnesota. "Those layers include everyone. The people who live out of town on farms and acreage. In-town locals. The people attracted to bicycling, the arts, theater. People connected to the churches. The Amish. Tourists. All those layers interlock and build strong community here."

You see local community happening at church worship services and potluck dinners. At "formal" settings like parent-teacher gatherings, town commissions, the Chamber of Commerce. Informal places, too, like the Legion, High Court Pub or Riverfront Saloon. On the Lanesboro Golf Course. Every Tuesday morning at the Cracked Egg Restaurant (formerly the Chat and Chew) nearly two dozen folks get together after yoga for coffee and conversation. (That's after the 6 a.m. guys coffee

"Lanesboro has a wonderful synergy created by the locals who live here and the tourists who visit here." (Lynn Susag)

bunch has left). Similar stuff is enjoyed each Friday morning at 9 a.m. when "The Dudes" gather at the Pastry Shop. Trivia Tuesdays brings people to the High Court Pub. So does Thursday's open mic night. The "Cocktail Club" convenes every six weeks or so.

"Community" isn't an official agenda item at meetings of the Lanesboro Community Theater planning group, the Lanesboro Writer's Group, a handful of local book clubs, the "44s" (we'll let the ladies in that club explain the name), the History Alive! actors-and-volunteers, or the Lanesboro Lodging Group. But community certainly happens at each of those. Nothing that happens in any of those gatherings (or others too new or numerous to mention) is more valuable, if you ask me.

Some of Lanesboro's best community is spontaneous. One email on a cold December afternoon convened two dozen carolers for an impromptu night of holiday singing at the senior apartments—followed, of course, with potluck. People here don't talk "community." They just do it.

Yesterday was Thanksgiving. More than 100 people gathered at the Discovery Faith Community (formerly the United Methodist Church) for a "Community Thanksgiving." Everyone is welcome, the meal (with all the traditional turkey fixings) is free. (Donations are collected for the local food shelf). It's a happy, warm, friendly time—it is community—and it's been happening for nearly 15 years now.

People in Lanesboro build community. It's too important not to.

Power Plant and old mill

The Spirit of Lanesboro:
People Here Care About Their Town

"Lanesboro is a hometown for the people who grew up here.
It becomes a hometown for the people who move here."
Mindy Gullickson

The fifth trait I see in the Lanesboro spirit is that people here care about their town. They like this place. They have a sense of ownership about it. They're proud to be a part of it. That goes for long-timers and newer folk. It just seems to happen.

Julie Kiehne lives outside of Lanesboro with her husband, Tim, who manages local grocery stores, and their kids (who will all graduate from its school). Julie is an original Rhubarb Sister and in the early 2000s served as Executive Director for the Chamber of Commerce. She knows this place very well.

The people of Lanesboro are definitely passionate about their town," she says. "They know there's something special and unique here. They want to help preserve that. That's the mark they want to make and the legacy they want to leave, to help sustain the magic that is Lanesboro."

One sign of that spirit is that volunteerism thrives here. People pitch in and help on all kinds of programs and projects, from riverside clean-ups to meals-on-wheels to community fundraisers to special events to downtown business promotions.

Lori Bakke is a shining example of that. "I grew up north of Lanesboro on our family farm," Lori says. "After high school I went away to college but I always knew I'd come back. This is home. This is the place I want to be."

Lori did come back, got married, and started her own family. She first opened a florist/gift shop business downtown called "Grandma's Garden," and today she owns and operates a family business in that same location called "Granny's Liquor." Lori loves it. She also loves taking an active part in Lanesboro. She has helped plan and guide Buffalo Bill Days for years, as well as the Christmas Dinner and downtown business promotions. She does all of that while taking care of her family and serving on nonprofit boards.

Volunteers bake 185 pies for Art in the Park each June.

"My mom was vice-president at the bank but she always found time to volunteer. I guess I'm following in her footsteps," Lori says. Why does she do it? "I care about Lanesboro," she says. "I want it to be successful. It's such a unique and friendly town. I love seeing good things happen here."

You find examples of community spirit like Lori's all around here. Lanesboro City Council meetings are well-attended. The Chamber of Commerce is active. Special-interest groups like business owners and lodging folks meet regularly. Discussions about a Lanesboro concept plan in 2016—thorough and spirited— were held in packed rooms. The Blandin Foundation's recent months-long training program for community volunteers had two dozen slots available. Twice that many people applied.

But if you really want to see community spirit in action, watch what happens in a crisis. That's been true many times in Lanesboro history. Fires and floods have been followed immediately by volunteers pitching in to get life back to normal. There's a great old photograph of volunteers gathering on Church Hill the day after the major fire of 1917 that destroyed the Lanesboro School and the Bethlehem Lutheran Church. The faces in that picture look sad and weary. But determined, too. Like they're ready to get to work to get things back to normal. That's exactly what they did.

On a Friday night last June volunteers were in Sylvan Park setting up booths and tables for Art in the Park was scheduled for the next day. Suddenly a fierce thunderstorm tore through town bringing high winds, rain and hail. Large trees and branches fell down in the Park, a key shelter was destroyed, roads were blocked, booths, tables and decorations were in shambles. The storm passed, followed by frantic phone calls. Should we cancel Art in the Park? That seemed to make the most sense.

Not in Lanesboro. Within the hour dozens of people showed up carrying chain saws, rakes, and shovels and started the clean-up. "People just came on their own," remembers Kara Maloney, Lanesboro Arts staff member. "It was amazing. They worked into the night using car headlights to help them see." Downed trees were removed, debris was cleared, booths were put back up. Art in the Park happened the next day and it was a total success, thanks to Lanesboro citizens who care about their town. "We couldn't have done it without them," said Kara. "They saved the day."

Six weeks later that spirit was again center stage. "Beautiful Something," a Coffee Street clothing-and-gift shop since 2015, caught fire on a Friday afternoon.

"People saw fire trucks and came from all over," says Shanalee Knight, the shop's owner. "People of all ages formed a line to help empty everything we could out of the shop. This was Lanesboro's Homecoming night. You knew people were busy. But they came anyway. We didn't know half of them, but they were all helping."

The building was saved, but sadly 100% of the store's inventory was destroyed by fire, soot and smoke. The help didn't end there, though. Pedal Pushers served dinner to the Knight family and donated their upstairs area to re-group. The Cozy Quilt shop next door offered space, and by the following weekend with re-ordered inventory Beautiful Something was back in business and making sales at the Girls Day Out event.

"Everyone's help here was wonderful," Shanalee says. "Lanesboro is like family."

This spirit of Lanesboro—the way people care about their hometown and put that into action—may be its most impressive and valuable shared trait. It doesn't mean there aren't challenges or that life here is always stress-free. People are people. Small towns are small towns. Tough discussions recently about protecting an historic town's unique character while promoting growth creates cross-currents, divergent viewpoints, even friction. That's fine. Even conflict can be a sign that people care. They'll figure it out and move on. That's been part of the Lanesboro spirit for a long time, too.

A recent mayoral race got tight. Emotions ran high. The Saturday after the election I volunteered at a riverside "clear the brush" project. Also helping were the defeated incumbent's wife and another lady who'd been his outspoken opponent. At one point, I saw the two women at opposite ends of a large log, working together to lift and carry it to the brush pile. I had to smile. Things do have a way of working out. Especially when everybody cares.

Norwegian Roald Amundsen, the first explorer to reach both the North and the South Poles and to cross the Northwest Passage, gave lectures in Lanesboro around 1903.

Lanesboro Says Goodbye to a Friend

"Every morning David woke up and fell in love with the world all over again."
Diane Knight

Y ou can attempt to define the spirit of Lanesboro. You can try to analyze it. It's better, though, to watch it in action. In a sad but powerful way that happened in the summer of 2017 when Lanesboro said goodbye to a friend.

Saturday, August 19, 2017

On a bright August morning I'm walking up Ridgewood Lane towards Church Hill. The sky is deep blue with a few white clouds. The summer air is already warm. The steeple of St. Patrick's Catholic Church rises high above me, and in it a single bell is slowly ringing. Each pell, clear and somber, echoes off the bluffs. Other people are walking up the Hill, too, and a line of cars is parking in the church lot. We're all on our way to the funeral mass for David J. Tacke of Lanesboro who passed last week at age 67 after a 30-year battle with a blood disease.

When David's condition was first diagnosed, doctors told him he could expect to live 5-10 more years. He beat that by 20. A quiet but energetic man with a passionate curiosity, David embraced life and lived it fully. He and his wife, Linda, raised two children, Paul and Greta. David became a respected IT specialist at the Minnesota Department of Revenue, an award-winning photographer, a talented chef, a naturalist, an environmental leader-writer-activist, a community volunteer, a musician, and a liturgist. Most important, David Tacke was a man loved by his family and valued as a friend. I walk into St. Patrick's, passing the acolyte still pulling the rope on that church bell, and I see the pews of this historic Lanesboro church packed with family and friends here to say goodbye.

David gave friendship as a quiet gift. "David met a lot of people, one at a time," Linda says. "But we all met the same David. He was interested in people. He asked questions and was a wonderful listener. That's how he connected best."

That describes my times with David. Our friendship was casual, our one-on-ones brief. I'd often see this tall, smiling man striding through town in his familiar hiking gear and floppy hat, camera in hand. When friends visited us from Minneapolis, I eagerly took them to David's studio to admire his stunning photography and to visit with this nice man. I enjoyed seeing David at the Friday morning Dudes breakfast. On one of those mornings last spring he told me about his upcoming trip to visit his son in Cairo, and his eyes brightened with excitement. But David asked about my family, too, and about our bed & breakfast. He listened to my answers.

I'll learn more about David today. And more about Lanesboro. David and Linda first came here years ago with their kids to bike and canoe. "The topography made us move here," Linda later tells me, with a laugh. "David loved the driftless region. He wanted to retire here and take lots of photos." They refurbished a condo in the historic Lanesboro School building, set up his studio, and after his retirement from his state job in 2012 made this their permanent home.

David quickly connected to the community. He also helped build it. He reached out to other local artists, naturalists, gardeners and chefs. A year-round biker and hiker, he loved being on the trail. He also loved and pursued music (he became St. Patrick's liturgist), environmental causes, and cooking. An invite to the Tacke table was a prized gift, given to many.

In the spring of 2017, David's illness—unexpectedly suppressed for so long through an extensive regimen of daily medicines—suddenly flared into a type of leukemia. He had to cancel that trip to Egypt and instead began new rounds of chemotherapy at Mayo. "David knew what he was facing," Linda says. "He did it head-on, in his steady, matter-of-fact way, just like he'd always done."

High fevers and low white-cell counts confined him to isolation at Mayo. Visits from Lanesboro friends weren't possible. Creative, can-do Lanesboro went into action. Word went out. David is sick, very sick. We need to let him know we're thinking about him. Let's meet in Sylvan Park. We'll make a video-message for him.

On short notice, with busy work schedules, perhaps only a handful of people will pull this off, but that's okay. On the day of the filming nearly 50 people showed up. (Remember, that's in a town of 750 people, a number that pretty much includes all kids and pets. An equivalent New York City turnout would be about one million.) They turned the video recorder on, people said "Hi, David!" waved handmade get-well signs, and sang boisterous versions of "Let Union Be" and "For He's a Jolly Good Fellow." It was joyful, heart-warming, overflowing with love, and filled with what Linda calls "that Lanesboro spunk."

David loved the video and watched it a number of times. He eagerly shared it with extended family members and friends, most of whom had no idea of what or where Lanesboro was. After seeing the video, one family member said, "I want to live there, too."

Another surprise was in store—David's health unexpectedly rallied. After it looked like he'd never leave the hospital, he was able to come home. June and July found him feel stronger and able to get out some. On Father's Day weekend he, Linda and Paul even drove to Grand Marais on Lake Superior to visit places he once photographed. One Friday morning all of us Dudes were happily shocked to see him walk into the Pastry Shop, with his big, casual smile.

David felt so good he did something Linda calls "classic David." To fulfill a donation-pledge to a Lanesboro nonprofit he and Paul prepared a full-course Egyptian-themed dinner for a dozen people at the Tacke home. The food was delicious (from chicken in Middle Eastern spices to baklava). Good wine and conversation flowed. No one enjoyed it more than David.

Nine days later this gifted, thoughtful, creative and kind man, was gone.

Now I'm one of hundreds at St. Patrick's saying goodbye. Last evening a rosary service was held here, too, followed by a root beer float "wake" hosted by local folks. (Home-made root beer, Arv's recipe, was donated by Pedal Pushers restaurant). Dozens of out-of-town relatives and guests needed Friday night lodging. On a busy summer weekend in Lanesboro B & Bs and hotels were all booked. Phone calls were made and people gladly opened their homes. "We housed 38 people and had still more offers coming in," says Linda. "It was amazing. I didn't even know most of the people who were helping." A cancellation opened one room at a B & B. "The room is yours, Linda, no charge," said the innkeeper. On Sunday morning more local helpers served breakfast to family and guests before the funeral service.

That service was beautiful and moving with music chosen by David, Linda and their friend, Rob Glover, a liturgist from their former parish in Deephaven. Father Ed McGrath's homily was personal and pointed. "David came to the end of his life with no fears and no regrets," he said.

After the service we all head to Eagle Bluff Learning Center for lunch and stories told by David's family and friends. His Air Force buddies from forty years ago traveled cross-country to attend. A Dudes "choir" adapted lyrics from the community theater's recent "Joseph" musical to honor their friend in song: "...there's one more angel in heaven, a beautiful star in the sky, David, we'll never forget you, it's tough but we're gonna get by." Paul closed by saying "...my dad had high expectations for himself. He quietly encouraged others to have high expectations for their lives, too." Handshakes and hugs, everyone walks out, pausing a final time to look at David's Scamp trailer and wooden canoe parked outside. This was all a sweet, sad goodbye for a gifted, loving man gone too soon but who lived life so well. David received much from this little town. He also gave much to it. Maybe that's the heart of the Lanesboro spirit. Giving and receiving. A two-way street that makes life better, for everyone.

Epilogue

Lanesboro Museum 2015

The Lanesboro History Museum opened in the Village Hall in 1976 and moved to its present location in 1984.

Lanesboro At 150

Two big anniversaries are a time to ask big questions.

Lanesboro is approaching two sesquicentennial celebrations. 2018 marks the 150th birthday of its rare and remarkable Stone Dam. 2019 will be the 150th anniversary of Lanesboro's incorporation as an official city. These anniversaries are great opportunities to highlight key events in town history and to celebrate the fact that Lanesboro has survived—thrived, even—in three different centuries. Quite an achievement!

Anniversaries are also good times to think about how things are going and where they're headed. How is Lanesboro doing? How's the local economy and business climate? Is population growing—or declining? What does the future hold for this town of fewer than 800 people? Is this community sustainable? Will Lanesboro celebrate its 200th birthday in 2068? If so, what will it look and feel like? More important, what do people want it to look and feel like?

Many rural towns in Minnesota don't make it to their 150th birthday. Agriculture creates an unpredictable, roller-coast economy. Small towns most often see their population decline. Young people graduate, go off to college, and don't return. Schools consolidate. Main street storefronts sit empty. The closing of the Post Office is often a major, devastating blow to a small, rural town. A few struggling businesses might remain, maybe a town museum with dusty, fading memories. The American rural landscape is sadly dotted with many "lost towns." Is that Lanesboro's fate?

I say no! My money is on Lanesboro to make it. This extraordinary little town, positioned so perfectly in an area of gorgeous natural beauty and resources, has so much going for it. A heritage of industrious, hard-working people. A solid agricultural base. The recreational assets of the Root River and the State Trail. People have been attracted to Lanesboro for well over a century now—residents and visitors alike. It seems hugely unlikely that its attraction will fade away.

There's no lock on that, though, no guarantees. Lanesboro is facing challenges that shouldn't be ignored. There are signs of aging in its century-old infrastructure. (The Lanesboro Dam itself is one example of that). The economic climate often

The Lanesboro High School class of 2016 had 22 graduates.

fluctuates, powerfully affected by state-wide and national forces beyond local control. (Ask folks who were around here during the Farm Crisis of the '70s or the Great Recession of 2008). No one can or should take for granted that Lanesboro's best days lie ahead.

"Lanesboro's magic isn't guaranteed," says Lyn Susag, Manager of the Cottage Street Inn. "What happens here has to be worked on and maintained. Look at the bike trail. Over the years people have worked hard and lobbied others to make sure it stays in great condition. None of that happens automatically."

In 2016 a community-wide effort asked important questions about the town's future. Surveys were taken, well-attended public forums were held, needs were identified, and priorities debated. Those efforts coalesced around the consultant work of Randall Arendt, a nationally-recognized expert in the field of rural and small-town development. Arendt visited Lanesboro, talked to its people, analyzed present conditions, and considered future needs and possibilities. In his summary report, he compared what he called "...this small (and) remarkable city" to an historic Victorian home. Over the last 50 years, Arendt wrote, "...the family in this 'house' has seen many of its children move away. A number of its rooms are no longer occupied...there are repairs that need to be made... (It) needs a lot of work...but (it) is basically sound and...attractive."

Arendt encouraged the town—its leaders, residents, everyone who cares about Lanesboro—to realize that critical decisions need to be made. A prioritized list of needed repairs must be identified. Planning and zoning issues need to be reviewed and updated as needed. And, just as important, new and larger income sources to fund repairs need to be discovered. "The future (can) look promising," Arendt concluded, "although everyone...must pull together and work hard to turn these dreams into reality."

Out of those discussions 17 priority areas were pinpointed. A handful of task forces have been named to move on some of them, with varying degrees of success to this point. Lanesboro isn't a "house" that will be renovated and refreshed overnight, everyone realizes that. But there are signs of energy and progress. And hope.

However these recent efforts go (the vision for this recent concept plan and other community "vision statements" remain the subject of discussion and debate), what isn't questioned is Lanesboro's spirit. People love this town. They get involved in it. The level of volunteer participation and energy here is remarkable. Like the river that runs through it, there's a momentum in this place that may rise and fall at times, but shows no signs of stopping.

Recent signs of energy and good news build optimism. The Minnesota Legislature—after years of hesitation and false starts—approved $4.6 million dollars in 2017 for repairs to the Lanesboro Dam to begin in the winter of 2018. A key downtown building, the old "blue hotel," which sat empty for years has new owners and the sound of hammers. Major renovation work has also begun on the Sons of Norway Lodge. Each year—thanks to DNR improvements and regular maintenance—the Root River Trail itself seems to get better and better.

Lanesboro, Minnesota, will soon hit 150. A time to look back, a time to celebrate, and a time to look ahead. Town founders were inspired to do great things here. Their vision, determination and hard work made it happen. Now it's our turn.

Why shouldn't the future of Lanesboro be just as bright, visionary and optimistic as the one envisioned by those first settlers? Yes, why not? Happy 150th birthdays, Lanesboro! Best wishes for 150 more.

Judge J. G. French by the Ingersoll Store

One More Trip
On the Lanesboro Road

"Keep your eyes on the road ahead and you'll see this beautiful
fairy tale village unfold in a breathtaking panorama..."
Minnesota Tour Brochure, 1880

We'll close our discovery of Lanesboro, Minnesota, where we began, with a ride down the County Road 8 hill into town from Fountain. This road has been here a long time in different forms. As old as the town itself, it has an inspiration all its own.

Some early travelers described the trip as fairy tale. Not everyone, though. M.G. Fellows, editor of a local newspaper here in the early 1900s, described his first trip down that road like this.

"Coming in sight of Lanesboro we beheld the village located along the river at the base of the bluff 300 feet below, the only way to get there being by a road excavated alongside of the bluff, too narrow for the passing of teams except in two or three places. I have crossed the Green Mountains of Vermont and the White Mountains of New Hampshire, but (approaching Lanesboro) I had never traveled over so perilous and unprotected a piece of highway."

Fellows ended by saying how happy he was to get safely off that hill and into a comfortable bed. It can still feel a bit like that on an icy winter night, for instance, but mostly this road is fairy tale, about 20 seconds of peaceful village, church steeples and bridges, a tree-lined park, a flowing river, a pocket-sized dam, all sitting—as someone else described it—in a limestone bowl. Even the water towers look good.

I'm not the only one mesmerized by this scene. I've heard many people refer to it as the first of their special Lanesboro memories. "I was driving into Lanesboro and I came down that hill..." is how those stories always start. People hit the words "came down that hill" and they smile, get a look in their eye, and you can see them searching for words to describe an experience, a feeling, that's difficult to put into words.

The County Road 8 road coming down into Lanesboro was once known as Duschee Hill.

We keep trying, though. Here's another one I've heard a number of times. "I came down that hill and it felt like I was driving into Brigadoon!" A village in an old Scottish tale, "brigadoon" has come to mean "...a place that's idyllic, unaffected by time, remote from reality." I can see why people use it. Lanesboro...Brigadoon. It fits.

But "Brigadoon" is mythical and Lanesboro isn't. It's a real place with a real history, and real people living out all the realities—ups, downs, joys, sorrows and foibles— of human life. We don't need to stretch the "brigadoon thing." But we can enjoy it. Even find some relaxing peace in it. In today's world, that's not a bad thing. We need more brigadoons.

The Lanesboro road is open. It takes you down, pulls you in, and leads you out again. I hope you've enjoyed the trip we've taken to Lanesboro's past, places and people. "Come back and see us, often," as they're fond of saying at the Commonweal. Come back down that road. Open yourself to Lanesboro and its series of simple pleasures. You'll be glad you did.

"Lanesboro, rich with wealth of bliss,
Where once these bluffs were rough and wild;
Where else has Nature ever smiled,
On more romantic scene than this?"

"Through all this district, secret little valleys branch off from the major valleys of the Root River (with) room enough and view enough for 11,000 poets." (Sinclair Lewis)

Appendix

Bethlehem Lutheran Church...early 1900s

Lanesboro Puzzlers

There's lots to look at and explore in Lanesboro. Some things to wonder about, too. Here are 20 Lanesboro puzzlers.

1. Who is Sylvan Park named after?

Somebody famous in the town's past? A Mr. Sylvan, no doubt? Good guess, but no. The Latin word "sylva" means "woods" (like in "Pennsylvania"). The Roman god "Sylva" was "god of the woods." In modern usage it's "a wooded place of natural beauty." That certainly fits. Sylvan Park was created on land donated by the Lanesboro Townsite Company and private citizens and has been a popular spot for town gatherings, concerts, family picnics, and camping for nearly 150 years.

2. Why is there a log cabin in Sylvan Park?

While we're in the neighborhood, what's that log cabin doing in Sylvan Park? It was built by the Lanesboro chapter of the Izaak Walton League in the late 1920s. The League, founded in 1922 and still an active conservation organization in the U.S., takes its name from the 17th century English author of "The Compleat Angler," the best-known book on fishing ever written. Lanesboro's chapter was established on June 6, 1925, with 38 charter members. The cabin has been secured and out-of-use for many years. So, another fun question: what's inside? Maybe some questions best remain mysteries.

3. Why is there a phone booth outside the Lanesboro History Museum?

Owned originally by (then) Ace Communications, this booth sat next to the telephone exchange building on Parkway Avenue since the 1950s, eventually becoming one of the most popular photo-op spots in town. ("Mommy, what's a phone booth?") Its still-working phone also led to creative prank-calls from pub patrons across the street to tourists tricked into answering it. ("Good afternoon. We need to inform you it's illegal to take pictures in Lanesboro.") Slated for removal in 2016, the booth was saved by locals who knew a treasure when they saw one and arranged for its new home. Its phone now offers brief recorded stories about Lanesboro told by residents and visitors. Give it a try. You won't even need a dime.

4. What are those medallions around town?

Twenty iron medallions scattered throughout Lanesboro create a fun "scavenger hunt" method of exploring the town. An iron pour in 2001 led by artists Coral Lambert and Karl Unnasch transformed donated metal objects like radiators and farm implements into unique symbols representing town history, landmarks, and points of interest. A decade later Unnasch (who lives in nearby Pilot Mound and who also designed the Commonweal Theatre's new look and lobby in 2007) organized a second pour to create additional medallions. A map and checklist is available at the Lanesboro Visitor Center and at Lanesboro Arts.

5. What's on top of the downtown Parkway street signs?

Lanesboro art shows up in unexpected places. Like on top of downtown street signs. A series of unique Wayfinding Signs was created by the above-mentioned award-winning sculptor and public artist Karl Unnasch and make getting around town just a little more fun. Look for a nut, an egg in a nest, and a berry as you stroll downtown on Parkway Ave.

6. What's that old sign with the globes hanging on Parkway Ave. near the Lanesboro Art Gallery?

That sign—slightly deteriorating but still vintage cool—marks the building that served as meeting hall of Lanesboro's International Order of Odd Fellows (I.O.O.F.) founded on May 28, 1869. A centuries-old fraternal and service organization dating back to 18th century England, the I.O.O.F. opened its first American order in Baltimore in 1819 and was the first U.S. fraternity to have both men and women members. Lanesboro's sign has three of its original six glass globes that highlighted its "triple links" motto of "Friendship, Love and Truth." Lanesboro's Odd Fellows disbanded in the mid-1900s.

7. Who is Henry Guttorsman?

Lanesboro's Legion Post # 40 was established in 1919 at the end of World War I and is named in honor of Henry M. Guttorsman from nearby Union Prairie who was killed in battle in France on August 6, 1918. Originally buried overseas, Guttorsman's remains were later returned to the United States and re-buried with honors near his family home.

8. What's that graffiti on the side of the Iron Horse?

The century-old red brick building on the northeast corner of Parkway Ave. and Coffee Street has housed a number of businesses and shops and is currently home to Iron Horse Outfitters and Inn. The Parkway side of the building displays graffiti left there for decades, including signatures from CCC boys in the 1930s that tell you their names, hometowns, even a few nicknames. See how many you can spot.

9. What's that tall structure across from the Stone Mills Suites?

Its fading painted sign identifies it as the "Lanesboro Grain Co., Grains-Feeds-Seeds," an elevator where farmers store and sell grain. It's been closed now for about ten years. Originally constructed around 1938, it had connections with the early founders of the Cargill Company that started in Wisconsin, Iowa and southern Minnesota in the 1870s. This elevator is currently home to "The Granary," a wine and beer bar (with ice cream and other goodies, too). A small section of railroad track is on the property, the last original rail line in Lanesboro. Two Lanesboro elevators—owned by the Horihan family—still operate, one in the Flat near the Sales Barn, the other on Highway 16 south of town, enduring and working symbols of Lanesboro's agricultural heritage.

10. Who are the Sons of Norway and why do they have a Lodge?

The Sons of Norway, the largest Norwegian organization outside of Norway, is a fraternal organization for people of Norwegian ancestry or interest. First established in Minneapolis in 1895, weekly dues assisted members in times of need. Eventually evolving into an insurance provider, early membership was restricted to men of Norwegian descent between 20-50 who were "morally upright, in good health, and capable of supporting a family." By 1900 a dozen similar lodges existed across the Midwest in towns with large Norwegian-American populations. Lanesboro's Sons of Norway #376 Heimbygda Lodge was established in 1929. In 1960 it purchased the Bethlehem Lutheran Church Hall, constructed in 1910. The Lodge is on the National Register of Historic Places and is still used for Sons of Norway meetings, musical concerts, and various community events. Major renovations to the building began in 2017, funded by Minnesota Historical Society grants and private contributions.

11. Why is there a wooden barber shop pole on 107 Coffee Street?

C.A. "Alf" Ward, a barber from Charles City, Iowa, moved to Lanesboro in 1878 to establish his business. A decade later Ward built a combination home-and-barber shop. That explains the pole. The house remained in the Ward family for 101 years. His son Bernard (one of four children who grew up in this house) became a barber, too, so people got haircuts from the Wards for 84 years! The family sold the building in the late 1980s and it became a rental space, spawning start-ups like "Windy Mesa," "Crown Trout Jewelers," and Marlin Miner's "Coffee Street Peddler." New owners in 2017 are planning the next chapter of this historic little shop with the wooden barber pole outside.

12. Does the outside burglar alarm on the bank building still work?

Photos of the Scanlan-Habberstad (now Merchants) Bank from the 1930s show this burglar alarm mounted on its outside north wall. The alarm was manufactured by the O.B. McClintock Company of Minneapolis, a maker of large public clocks and bank alarms during the first half of the 20th century. Thousands of banks across the country had McClintock alarms with bells activated by push buttons located in the bank's vault and at each teller cage. The clanging could be heard blocks away, it was said. This alarm is no longer operational today, but maybe just having it up there will make potential bad guys think twice. Not that we have any of those in Lanesboro.

13. Is there still a fall-out shelter in the bank?

Yes and no. A metal, gold-and-silver fall-out shelter sign, with its now iconic three-triangles-in-a-circle logo, is still bolted to the Parkway Avenue side of Merchants Bank. It went up in the duck-and-cover days of the early 1960s when getting ready for a nuclear blast was considered good planning. The shelter was the bank's large basement, home to its original vault and a large stone cistern. No one recalls supplies or emergency equipment being stored there, but it offers a sturdy shelter during tornado and storm warnings.

14. What is the Bunny Trail?

On Sylvan Park's northern edge is a dirt trail up Church Hill originally built by CCC boys in the 1930s. Known as the "Bunny Trail," it was a popular walking route for Lanesboro kids going back-and-forth to school and church activities. When the Lanesboro School moved to Brooklyn, the trail fell into disrepair. Recent volunteers and donations (including local student groups, Sentence to Service crews, and materials from Bruening Rock Products) are bringing the Bunny Trail back to life. (I can't think of that trail without remembering a story Curt Austin—then in his 90's—told me about what it was like to grow up in Lanesboro in the 1930s. He shared how the boys in his elementary class walked up that trail to school in the morning, each of them carrying a .22 rifle for squirrel hunting after school. A different time, a different world.)

15. Why are some Lanesboro homes made out of cement blocks?

Lanesboro has a number of beautiful and historic homes. A handful are unique because they're made out of cement blocks. First designed in Europe more than a century ago, concrete block houses are solid, sturdy, and well-insulated against temperature and noise. Why were they built in Lanesboro? They made sense in Minnesota's extreme climate and the Habberstad Block Factory in the Flat neighborhood in the early 1900s (owned by Ole Habberstad) made blocks available and affordable. You'll find examples at 708 and 716 Kenilworth Ave. S. the corner of Ashburn St. and Park Avenue N. and , and 203 Kenilworth Ave. N.

16. Where and what is Inspiration Point?

Inspiration Point is a scenic overlook on Highway 16 between Lanesboro and Preston that provides wonderful views of the Root River Valley and a fully-accessible picnic area. Those busy CCC boys worked on this, too, from 1934-1937. A $1.8 million dollar restoration/improvement project on the Point was completed in 2015 by the Minnesota Department of Transportation. A great spot to take a break—and get inspired.

17. What are the pictures on the side of the Pedal Pushers building?

Those mosaics, created by St. Paul artist Bailey Cahlander, went up in the summer of 2017, funded by the Jerome Foundation. Their aqua-themed designs portray river scenes and were created to complement the Smithsonian "Waterways" exhibit that came to town that same year. Lanesboro folk were hands-on volunteers, donating glass pieces, cutting and breaking glass, and gluing bits of glass onto Beth's design. A work of art that everyone can be proud of.

18. Why does the town whistle always blow at noon?

Many rural Minnesota towns—including Lanesboro—have a siren that goes off every day at noon. Years ago those loud blasts signaled factory and shop workers that it was time for lunch. The same siren warns people about approaching storms and alerts first responders to fires or emergencies. (Makes you wonder what happens if a big catastrophe ever hits exactly at noon). Many small towns—again including Lanesboro—periodically receive requests to silence the noon whistle. For many reasons, mostly tradition and nostalgia, that hasn't happened yet. Probably won't. "I want to live in a town that blows a noon whistle," a fellow Lanesboro resident says. I know exactly what he means.

19. Why does Lanesboro have two old bridges so close together?

Bridges have always played a pivotal role in Lanesboro, a town with a river (the Root) running through it. Early wooden bridges coming off the west bluff were regularly battered, a few even destroyed during big storms and floods. In 1893 a steel bridge built by the Chicago Bridge Company was put in place. ("The new iron bridge will fill a long-felt want," said a resident at the time. "We hope it will stay by us longer than the other ones did.") It certainly did. In 2003, slated for replacement, the bridge became a picturesque "walking bridge" at the intersection of Coffee Street West and Rochelle Ave North.

20. Why is that eagle on the pole by the Bass Pond?

There are many eagles around Lanesboro. You'll see them soaring overhead or sitting in trees high above the Root River looking for fish. One eagle sits stoically, majestically even, on a tall pole next to the Bass Pond. Why does he sit there so still for so long? Because he's not real. Don't feel bad if you get fooled, though. It happens to pretty much everyone around here. He sits there to scare away Canada geese.

Jerre Allis of Old Barn fame sold "Tommy Britton," his champion trotter horse, to a California breeder for $150,000.

10 More Bluff Country Treasures

Lanesboro offers more than enough to see, do and enjoy, but if you find yourself with some extra time (or maybe a rainy day) here are ten more bluff country places and events worth checking out.

1. Niagara Cave (Harmony) and Mystery Cave (Forestville State Park)

Both casual cave fans and serious spelunkers will be happy to learn about two local public caves. Niagara Cave near Harmony, discovered in 1924 by a farmer looking for three lost little pigs, is rated one of the top 10 cave attractions in the U.S. and welcomes more than 30,000 visitors yearly. It has a 60-foot underground waterfall (that's where its name comes from), spectacular rock formations probably millions of years old, and even a subterranean wedding chapel. Wear comfortable shoes (you'll climb 250 steps) and layered clothes (the cave is 48 degrees year-around). In 2015 it became the first public cave in the world whose energy use is 100% solar-powered. A gift shop and mini-golf, too. The Mystery Cave at Forestville State Park, between Preston and Spring Valley offers a ¾ mile walking path and guided tours, including a lantern tour, a geology tour, a wild caving tour, a photography tour and more.

2. Historic Forestville (near Preston)

Historic Forestville, a restored "living museum" operated by the Minnesota Historical Society, presents the story of an authentic pioneer town of the 1850s that at its peak had a grist mill, a school, two hotels, a saw mill, a general store and more. You can visit Thomas Meighen's General Store, see original merchandise, and learn first-hand from costumed guides about everyday life in a town that eventually disappeared but left a fascinating trace.

3. Ed's Museum (Wykoff, 17 miles from Lanesboro on County Road 8)

Ed Krueger lived all his 91 years in Wykoff, graduated from Wykoff High, married there and raised a family, was town treasurer for decades, and ran the weekly silent pictures at the A-MUZ-U Theater. His main gig was running the Jack Sprat Grocery Store from 1933 to 1989. On his passing, Ed donated the store and its remaining merchandise to the town. You can browse store shelves still stocked with original items—including unopened pop bottles, candy bars and cereal boxes—and everything else Ed collected, which was a lot: original movie posters, magazines (every TV Guide from 1954), his

1920s metal toys, rock collections, the door downstairs with a peephole (part of the building's speakeasy past), a tarantula Ed found in a box of bananas, even his deceased cat Sammy in a (thankfully) tightly-sealed cardboard box. The family apartment upstairs offers a peek into his son's 1950s bedroom filled with original toys and clothes. Another fun step back in time.

4. The Norsland Lefse Factory in Rushford

Southeastern Minnesota is the heart of Norwegian history and culture in the U.S. What's more Norwegian than lefse? This traditional flatbread made of potatoes, flour, salt, and vegetable oil (think Scandinavian tortilla) is a traditional holiday treat but tastes good all year. People put many things on lefse: butter, sugar, cinnamon, lingonberries, jelly, even peanut butter. You can also roll it up with eggs, meat, spreads, and cheeses. You can get lefse year-round at the Norsland Lefse Factory in Rushford (18 miles from Lanesboro on Highway 16). You can also watch them make it at their in-store factory, now in its 25th year. (There's a bakery, sandwich and gift store here, too). Norsland produces more than 500,000 "rounds" of lefse each year for distribution across the U.S. Feeling brave? Kick your Uff Da up a notch and try a little lutefisk.

5. The Old Barn Resort

Located near the Root River State Trail between Lanesboro and Fountain, the Old Barn Resort offers campgrounds, overnight hotel/hostel accommodations, a swimming pool, tubing and fishing gear rentals, a bar/restaurant, and an 18-hole golf course, all located on a beautiful, historic farm setting dominated by—you guessed it—a huge white barn.

That four-story barn has quite a history. Edward Allis, a Milwaukee farm equipment manager of Allis-Chalmers fame, purchased this former mill site in the now-lost town of Clear Grit in January, 1882. His son, Jere, ran the farm, raising hogs and Holsteins and adding this barn with enough room for 75 cattle. He later acquired an interest in trotter horses, owning 20 at one time. The farm's two race tracks became the site of elaborate social gatherings, dances, and summer picnics. Skiing and ice skating were popular in the winter. In 1889 Edward Allis died and Jere's marital problems led to his selling the property to land speculators in 1906 for only $15,000. A century later Vernon Michel bought it and transformed it into the Old Barn Resort, a popular family vacation destination adjacent to the Root River State Trail.

6. Fore! Golfing in Bluff Country

Golfers can tee it up around here at public courses in just about every small town, including Lanesboro, Harmony, Chatfield, Preston, and Rushford. Courses here feature beautiful bluff-country landscapes and are less crowded than big city counterparts. Reasonably-priced green fees, too.

Lanesboro Golf Course
900 Parkway Ave S, Lanesboro, MN 55949
(507) 467-3742

Preston Golf Course
MN-16, Preston, MN 55965
(507) 765-4485

Rivers Bend at Old Barn Resort
24461 Heron Rd, Preston, MN 55965
(507) 467-2512

Harmony Golf Club
545 4th St NE, Harmony, MN 55939
(507) 886-5622

Ferndale Country Club
23239 MN-16, Rushford, MN 55971
(507) 864-7626

Chosen Valley Golf Club
1801 Main Street, Chatfield, MN 55923
(507) 867-4305

7. Stand Still Parade in Whalan

Every third Saturday of May, Whalan, Minnesota, (population 63), about 4 miles east of Lanesboro on Highway 16, has a parade. An unusual parade. It remains stationary while spectators walk around, in front of, behind, sometimes even through it. This is a "stand still parade" for good reason. Whalan's main street is barely three blocks long. If there's going to be a parade here, this is the only way it can happen.

It's a full-fledged parade, mind you. The grand marshal sits in a parked antique car (last year a 1932 Duisenberg) right behind the veterans honor guard that sits in folding chairs hoisting American flags. Fire trucks, floats, a high school (standing, not marching) band, horses, a local politician or two—it's all here. It's just not going anywhere. Kids walk up to the floats to get candy. A day-long festival prolongs the fun, offering crafters, family games, and fair food with a Norwegian twist. (Hot dogs, but rommegrot and lefse, too). This is Minnesota so you'll find pies, bars and cookies from the ladies of the Whalan Lutheran Church. Live music (the Rutabaga Brothers are always a big hit) and a pie-eating contest (with donations from Whalan's popular Aroma Pie Shoppe) are highlights. Big, happy crowds love this parade and return every year. (www.standstillparade.org.)

8. Owl Center in Houston

The Houston Nature Center and International Owl Center, located 30 miles southeast of Lanesboro at the eastern end of the Root River trail, has an international reputation for its owl programs and annual International Festival of Owls held the first weekend in March. The Center's mission is to "advance the survival of wild owl populations through education and research." That happens through a variety of exhibits and programs that teach people about these nocturnal birds of legend and lore. If you have even a slight interest in owls and "who" doesn't (sorry), you won't be disappointed.

9. Pie! Pie! Pie!

There's almost a spiritual connection between people and pie in Minnesota. (I say "Betty's," you say what?). Bluff country more than holds its own with great local pie-makers and pie shops. Three of our family favorites: The Aroma Pie Shop in Whalan (618 Main Street, 507-467-2623), Burdey's Café in Peterson (417 Mill Street, 507-875-2424) and the Village Square in Fountain (99 Main Street, 507-268-4406). All three are on the Root River State Trail. Pie Crawl, anyone?

10. Minnesota Marine Art Museum in Winona

The river city and college town of Winona, 40 miles from Lanesboro, a scenic 51-minute trip, is home to the Minnesota Marine Art Museum (MMAM). "Expect to be surprised," the MMAM says. You will be. The museum opened in 2006 with a primary focus on traditional maritime art but has expanded to include originals from European and American masters, including Picasso, Van Gogh, Monet, Gauguin,

Cézanne, Turner, Constable, Leutze, O'Keeffe, Cassatt, Homer, Cole, and Wyeth. Another popular draw is the museum's extensive collection of folk art from popular regional sculptor and artist, Leo Smith. A pretty river view, too.

I know I said 10, but...if you're in Winona anyway and you appreciate the look, feel and aroma—never mind the goodies—of an old-fashioned bakery, swing by Bloedow's where people have been lining up daily for fresh-baked donuts, pastries and breads since 1924. (451 E. Broadway Street, (507) 452-3682)

George Dolpin, captain in a "negro regiment" of the Union Army, was named commander of Lanesboro's Grand Army of the Republic post in 1905.

About the Illustrator

Lisa Gaunky is the talented artist who created the beautiful illustrations in this book. Lisa makes her home near Sparta, Wisconsin, with her husband, David, and daughter, Belinda, on a little piece of heaven they like to call the "Pine Grove Supper Club and Bait Shoppe." Lisa has written and illustrated other books, including "The Illustrated History of Sparta." In her spare time she spreads the joy of literacy in her local school system, helps guide the Sparta Farmer's Market, and works on her love of illustration.

For more information about Lisa's work, including the illustrations in this book that are available in both prints and cards, she can be reached at:

Lisa Gaunky
wildberrystudio@ymail.com

Acknowledgements

Chip and Jean Borkenhagen

Chip, we sat together one summer afternoon in the lobby of an Aitkin, Minnesota, tire shop, working on this book, one day after your latest chemo round, two hours after my minor eye surgery. We must have enjoyed this project. I know working with you and Jean has been a total joy. You're a champion and an inspiration, my friend. Thanks for delivering on your promise of a beautiful book.

Lisa Gaunky

Years ago Susie and I walked into a cozy little gift shop in Sparta, Wisconsin, picked up a book called "Illustrated Sparta" and immediately loved its beautiful line drawings. "Lanesboro could use a book like this," Susie said. "Who's the illustrator?" I asked the friendly shopkeeper. "That would be me," you said with a smile. From there we are here. Thank you, Lisa, for the exquisite quality of your work, your patience, your encouragement, and your friendship. All that and we got to meet Dave and Belinda, too—what a deal!

Don Ward

His name should rhyme with "Lanesboro history." He loved his hometown and its history and his thorough and passionate efforts in collecting its history gave this town a priceless gift. Thank you, Don (and Theo St. Mane) for your excellent work on the book "Images of Lanesboro" that captures this town so well in text and vintage photographs and that served as a key resource for this book.

Special thanks to Sandy Webb

Executive Director of the Lanesboro History Museum. Lanesboro history oozes out of every corner of that neat old building on Parkway and Sandy (with her staff and volunteers) do a wonderful job of keeping it organized, accessible, and attractive.

One of the simple but great pleasures in writing a book about Lanesboro is meeting and talking with so many nice and interesting people. Helpful, too. Thanks to the following (apologies, please, if I missed anyone):

Vern Riddle, Joan Finnegan, Julie Kiehne, Michele Peterson, Jane Peck, Rick Lamon, Phil and Heidi Dybing, Carol Person, Tom Manion, Marlin Miner, Alton Peterson, Sara Torkelson, Robert (Bob) Olson, Dave Applen, Bill and Karen Swanson, Dave Harrenstein, Brenda Chiglio, Donna Sveen, Robin and Bethany Krom, Julia Borgen, Jeremy van Meter, Catherine Glynn, Scott and Angie Taylor, Carla Noack, Gene and Renee Bergstrom, Dennis and Mary Kelly, Robin Edmiston, Ed Taylor, Autumn Johnson, John Davis, Peggy Hanson, Frank Wright, Jeff Green, Hal Cropp, Cheryl Krage, Jack and Nancy Bratrud, David Hennessey, Dave and Lynn Susag, Caleb and Blake Lauritsen-Norby, Robbie Brokken, Gordon and Val Tindall, Jennifer Wood, Beth Hennessy, Kara Maloney, Jeff Kam, Nancy Martinson, Cliff and Jane Grevstad, Marv and Carol Eggert, Adam Wiltgen, Darla Taylor, Tom McGuigan, Peter and Vickie Torkelson, Jim Warburton, the late Orval Amdahl, Mary Bell, Eliza Mitchell, Kate O'Neary, JoAnne Agrimson, Mark and Elaine Edwards, the late Curt Austin, Rick Haugen, Don Bell and Anna Looney, Bob Thomas, Ceil Allen, Pete and Barbara Benson (Bebe) Keith, Jerry and Rita Dalzell, Mai Gjere, Olivia Obritsch, Nora Sampson, Laurie Bakke, Linda Schomburg Tacke, the late David Tacke, Karen Miller, Robin Pearson, Dick and Diane Haight, and Candace Simar.

Index

Lanesboro's Legion building, built in 1873 and originally a millinery, is the oldest Legion building in the United States.

For more information about Lanesboro, Minnesota, including business, lodging, theater, and restaurant guides, please visit:

www. Lanesboro.com

For additional copies of this book–"Lanesboro, Minnesota" by Steve Harris–contact Steve at sharrislb@gmail.com or call (952) 836-7904.